BLAIRSVILLE SENIOR HIGH SCHOOL
BLAIRSVILLE, PENNA.

DATE DUE

On to Kilimanjaro

By the author of

THE BIG PUSH:
A PORTRAIT OF THE BATTLE OF THE SOMME

Brian Gardner

ON TO KILIMANJARO

The Bizarre Story of the First World War
in East Africa

MACRAE SMITH COMPANY: Philadelphia

*To those who fought and died in
Africa in the First World War
unnoticed by the rest of the world.*

ACKNOWLEDGMENTS

I am indebted to the following:

Messrs. Faber and Faber for extracts from *Trekking On* by Deneys Reitz; Messrs. Hurst and Blackett for extracts from *My Reminiscences of East Africa* by General von Lettow-Vorbeck; The Controller of H.M. Stationery Office for extracts from *History of the Great War, Military Operations, East Africa,* Vol. I; Messrs. Methuen for extracts from *With the Nigerians in German East Africa* by W. D. Downes; Messrs. John Murray for extracts from *Three Years of War in East Africa* by A. Buchanan, *Sketches of the East Africa Campaign* by R. V. Dolbey, and *The Gold Coast Regiment in the East Africa Campaign* by Sir Hugh Clifford; Colonel R. Meinertzhagen and Messrs. Oliver and Boyd for extracts from *Army Diary, 1899–1926;* Messrs. H. F. & G. Witherby for extracts from *The East African Field Force* by C. P. Fendall.

The Imperial War Museum, Messrs. Hurst and Blackett, the Gresham Publishing Co. and Colonel R. Meinertzhagen for illustrations in this book.

Mr. Thomas Muir, of Goring-by-Sea, Sussex, who was attached to the K.A.R. during the campaign, for his advice and for reading, checking and commenting on this account.

The spelling of place names is generally
that in common use at the time.

CONTENTS

CONTENTS

INTRODUCTION

THIS is the story of a little-known campaign. While the great blood-bath of the Western Front, in the First World War, is imprinted on the minds of men forever, few people know much of the campaign in East Africa in that same war. Few reports of the fighting went home at the time. History books written since, and general accounts of the war, have dismissed it in a few sentences if they have even mentioned it at all.

And yet the war in German East Africa was a fascinating one. It would be difficult to imagine anything further removed from the dreary, stark years of horror of the war in Europe. This was a war of a totally different kind. A war of adventure and initiative, of open movement and small units, of wits and of heroism. Parts of it might have been taken from the pages of a novel by G. A. Henty.

It was fought over immense distances, sometimes over un-explored and unmapped areas, in jungles where man-eating lions were often a worse danger than the enemy, in deadly swamps and on remote mountains; in a tropical climate where disease had hardly begun to be conquered, when tropical medicine was still in its infancy. One of the many extraordinary aspects of the campaign was the conglomeration of different races that fought side by side in a comparatively small army—Sikhs, Punjabis, Arabs, West Indians, Rhodesians,

Sudanese, Nigerians and members of many East African tribes, as well as Afrikaners, English, Irish, Scots and Welsh. Although there were only two battalions of the British Army involved, many other Britons were engaged; in the Royal Navy, in the Indian Army and the King's African Rifles (K.A.R.), and in the auxiliary services.

A good deal of the campaign in "German East" and the surrounding territories is unknown, and always will be. Many of the units kept no records at all for long periods. Even the daily war-diary kept at British G.H.Q. contains little information. On the German, Belgian and Portuguese sides, affairs were so much a matter of local initiative, thousands of miles away in jungle and bush, that it must have seemed absurd to keep records of forays and remote battles. Combatants were too busy locating enemy patrols and forts—as well as their own positions—and warding off malarial mosquitoes, tsetse flies, "jigger-fleas," which burrow into men's feet and leave them crippled, termites, scorpions, rhinos, centipedes, poisonous giant spiders, fierce hornets and warrior ants. Even the British *Official History of the War* has given up after one volume, covering half the campaign. Recently, a little more has come to light. But many of the details of this story are lost forever.

To those fighting in East Africa, unnoticed by the rest of the world, it must have seemed almost a private affair. Perhaps that is why some courtesies of war from a bygone age, trampled into the mud in Europe, managed to survive in German East. It is a war that deserves, perhaps, to be better known, for not only does it contain many tales of individual heroism and adventure, but it saw also a great disaster that for military bungling has possibly never been surpassed in British history, a miniature naval struggle in the heart of a continent, and in its closing stages it becomes a story of such extraordinary endurance and defiance on both sides that even war itself becomes almost ennobled. It saw, also, the fulfilment of two remarkable soldiers, one a British intelligence officer and one a German colonel, and the nadir of the career of one of the great leaders of the first half of the century.

Inevitably, this book is garnered from others that have been written before; each dealing with an aspect or part of the campaign, most of them written by men who were there. The result is, as it were, a montage—the first general account of the whole of this campaign from the point of view of both sides. Some small actions and columns have been omitted. Information about them is scanty; much of it inaccurate—even official records being now recognized as frequently doubtful and misleading.

Instead of a detailed account, week by week, a more general picture has been attempted—one that includes the atmosphere as well as the facts of World War I in Africa.

On to Kilimanjaro

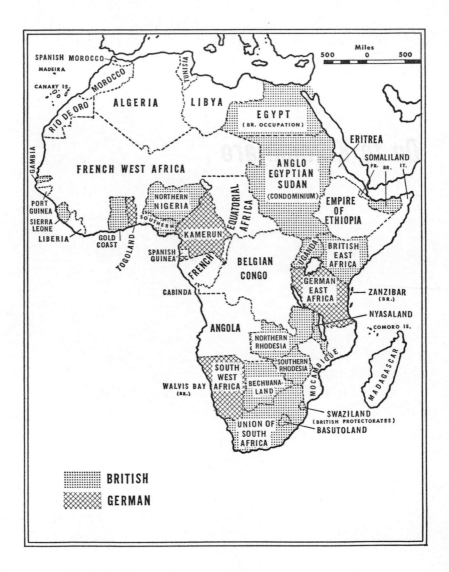

Africa at the outbreak of World War I (1914).

Chapter 1

A PLACE IN THE SUN

July, 1914, was one of the happiest months Dar-es-Salaam, the seaport town which served as capital of German East Africa, had known since the arrival of the Germans some decades before. The final length of the great railway running west to Ujiji on Lake Tanganyika had just been completed after months of frustrating engineering difficulties and native troubles. Shortly there was to be a ceremonial opening and an exhibition. There were many visitors from Germany, sipping drinks with friends in the small hotels and on the verandas of private houses on the slopes behind the town. Everyone was confident of the great future in store for the colony; especially in the matter of commercial profits. Dhows idled in the harbor as the sun set with almost overwhelming beauty. Traders, for the first time, were beginning to feel the comfort of promised and certain wealth.

As well as visitors from the Fatherland, planters from the surrounding country and from the settled northern area of the colony had flocked into the town for the railway celebrations.

In the Officers' Club, where the whirring fans did their best to subdue some of the oppressive heat, one man sat in a cane chair, quietly writing notes and contemplating the scene. Putting the notes in the pocket of his white jacket, he would sometimes join a party for a game of bridge. Later, he would leave the Club and stroll, almost unnoticed, to the post office where he would have a chat with a clerk.

This man was Norman King, British Consul stationed in Dar-es-Salaam. King sent off to London frequent reports on conditions in the colony and on such matters as the relative fighting value of Europeans in different districts. He considered that the well-fed citizens of Dar-es-Salaam would, in the event of hostilities, have "little stomach for fighting" in behalf of Germany. Their main concern would be to avoid anything that interrupted their prospects of making quick but sizeable fortunes. It is doubtful if anyone at that time paid much attention to the investigations and reports of this conscientious but somewhat remote consular official. His reports were no doubt placed in some file and quickly forgotten in the wake of more important matters. But some of them were later to be useful.

There was one man in Dar-es-Salaam, however, who noticed the quiet Englishman; who observed his note-taking in the Club and his visits to the post office. For, sitting across the clubroom, surrounded by young officers and prominent local citizens, was, on many a long hot afternoon, the new German Commander-in-Chief of East Africa, Colonel Paul von Lettow-Vorbeck. And he, among other qualities, was a notably perceptive man.

A tallish figure, with a small but firm jaw; thin, tight lips; a long, sloping forehead and close-cropped hair, he looked like a British caricature of a Prussian officer. He was not popular in Dar-es-Salaam. For one thing, he was a newcomer who seemed to think he knew better about local affairs than people who had spent years in the colony. And although he was no more arrogant than any other senior officer of his day, he did seem to carry conceit a little far.

In fact, the only time von Lettow-Vorbeck had seen the place before was when he had been wounded in an uprising in German West Africa and the ship that was bringing him home called at the port. The son of a general and forty-four years old, he had spent his whole life in the army, to the honor of which he was even more attached than he was to Germany. He was an admirer of Caesar's *Gallic War*. He had been an expert on colonial matters for the German General Staff; had fought in China in 1900–1, when he had become friendly with the British officers also engaged there; and had experienced two years of bush warfare during the Hottentot Rebellion of 1904 (only South African commanders could outmatch this, as it turned out, invaluable experience). At this time he had made many friends among the Boers and had studied their military methods, especially those of Botha (to whose staff he was for a time seconded). Later, he had become commander of the Marines at Wilhelmshaven, which had given him some knowledge of naval matters and an insight into broader strategy. He had taken part in an official visit to Norway, had then commanded the force in the Cameroons, and by 1914 had enjoyed a more varied experience than probably any other German officer, having taken part in naval maneuvers in large and small ships, bush fighting, combat in China and a great deal of mixed staff and regimental duties. Precisely why he was sent

[19]

to a distant and strategically unimportant sphere before the outbreak of a European war remains a mystery.

Lettow-Vorbeck spent much of the early part of 1914 on a tour of inspection in the northern area, close to the border of British East Africa. He traveled by sea to Tanga from Dar-es-Salaam and then up the rail track to Moshi. He leisurely visited plantations, learned about the country and, above all, the Africans—how to treat them, what they respected, what they despised and who they would follow and why. He gossiped in the shade of verandas with old friends of his youth, whom he had known as a cadet. At one estate he enjoyed the home-grown coffee; at another the Moselle. He shot for buffalo, with little success. He and his party were even attacked by some native warriors, complete with war-dress, ostrich feathers, blood-curdling war-cries and spears. Eventually, he fell into a rocky hole and got water on the knee.

As for war with the English, most people, including Colonel von Lettow-Vorbeck, thought it highly unlikely and felt that Germany was "on exceptionally good terms with the English," as he himself said. Europe seemed a long, long way away and it was not easy to understand what one heard of affairs there.

Of all the European countries to enter the "Scramble for Africa," Germany was the last. It owed the possessions it had there by the start of the 1914 war more to commercial enterprise than to the efforts of nationalist explorers or military conquest. Its colony in East Africa, the jewel of the German Colonial Empire, was nearly as large as Germany and France combined.

The early pioneer work was done through private enterprise, mainly by the German Colonization Society. Only when these pioneers had achieved some success in bringing German influence to the area did Bismarck step in and accord them official recognition and support. Not until Lord Salisbury's brief succession to the British Foreign Office in 1885 had the place become so settled as to warrant an official recognition of the various spheres of European influence. A commission was set up, with German, British and French representatives (the British representative was the future Lord Kitchener), and five years later, in 1890, boundaries were drawn. These gave Britain a protectorate over the islands of Zanzibar, but Germany was granted what became known as German East Africa, or Tanganyika today; the Sultan of Zanzibar having ceded much of the territory, over which he had little, if any, control, for four million marks. The northern boundary of the German territory was through an area little known and in parts unexplored (although legend had it that it could best be traced by following the empty Vermouth bottles discarded by the Anglo-German boundary commission—Vermouth being a local preventive for blackwater fever). In the early 1890s, Britain increased its holdings to Nyasaland and the northern areas of Rhodesia.

Germany had thus acquired an area, bounded by sea, lakes and British, Belgian and Portuguese territory, about 700 miles from south to north and 600 miles east to west. In the early years of the twentieth century the German settlers continued, together with their neighbors, in the long and arduous task of developing their colony, or "protectorate," and subduing the natives, most of whom had never heard of Lord Salisbury and were not aware that they were now so fortunate as to be under German rule. In 1898, the British fought disgruntled tribes in Nyasaland. The Germans were doing so in German East on the eve of the outbreak of war. In 1914, the K.A.R. (King's African Rifles) were engaged in a war ("a punitive expedition") against tribes in northeast Uganda, at that time unmapped.

There were about eight million natives in German East, and five thousand Europeans (including several hundred Boers who had settled there, preferring German to British rule).

The country was being opened up from two railway lines. One was from the port of Tanga in the north, to Moshi at the foot of Kilimanjaro—the Usambara Railway, 270 miles long; and the other from the port and capital of Dar-es-Salaam to Lake Tanganyika—the Central Railway, 780 miles long (a remarkable engineering achievement across some of the wildest parts of Africa). The centers of civilization were along these railways, in the pleasant climate in the foothills of Kilimanjaro and in the various harbors along the coast. Apart from this the country, especially the southern area, was still entirely undeveloped by 1914.

Early in August, von Lettow was again out in the back country, having recovered from his knee, at Kilosa, about 200 miles up the railway line from Dar-es-Salaam. There,

---

Allied Invasions of German East Africa, 1916–17.

1. Crewe (British), July–Sept., 1916
2. Tombeur (Belgian), July–Sept., 1916
3. van Deventer (British), March, 1916–Jan., 1917
4. Tighe & Malleson (British), March, 1916
5. Northey (British), July, 1916–Feb., 1917
6. Invasion of Seaports (British), Sept., 1916
7. Gil (Portuguese), Sept., 1916

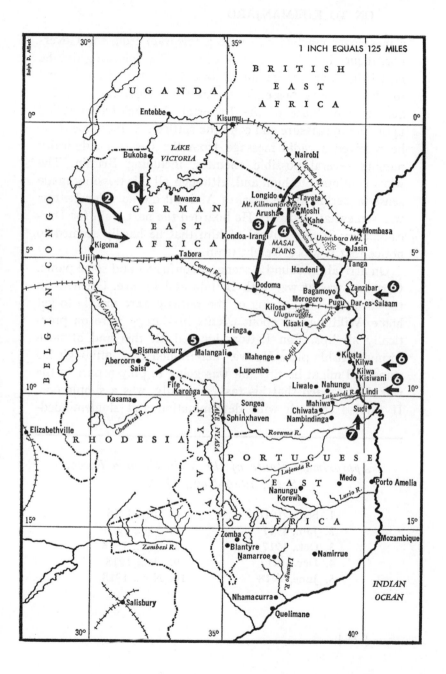

a messenger reached him with a telegram from the Governor, requesting his immediate return. The following day he heard that war was imminent, but that it would not extend to the overseas possessions. Another telegram from the Secretary of State of the Imperial Colonial Office called upon him to reassure and calm the settlers. At the same time, he received a radio message from the German Admiralty naming several possible enemies, including Britain. The wires continued to hum and, although all this possibly made sense in Berlin, in the heart of Africa it did not. Von Lettow was somewhat confused. He boarded the next train for Dar-es-Salaam; it was typical of him that he hardly seemed to notice that it was a freight train.

On arrival, he found a scene of confusion and some panic. Germany was at war with Britain and France. Germans in the town for the opening of the railway were unable to get home. Wild rumors about events in Europe were on practically all lips. Von Lettow ignored all this and at once formulated his plan. He was determined that, although his command might be tiny, he was going to play a part in the war. He realized that his task, basically, was a simple one. If carried through with determination and singleminded-

---

Approximate Route of the Main German Force,
Sept., 1916–Nov., 1918.

1. Sept., 1916	6. July, 1918
2. Jan., 1917	7. Aug., 1918
3. Oct., 1917	8. Sept., 1918
4. Dec., 1917	9. Oct., 1918
5. June, 1918	10. Nov., 1918

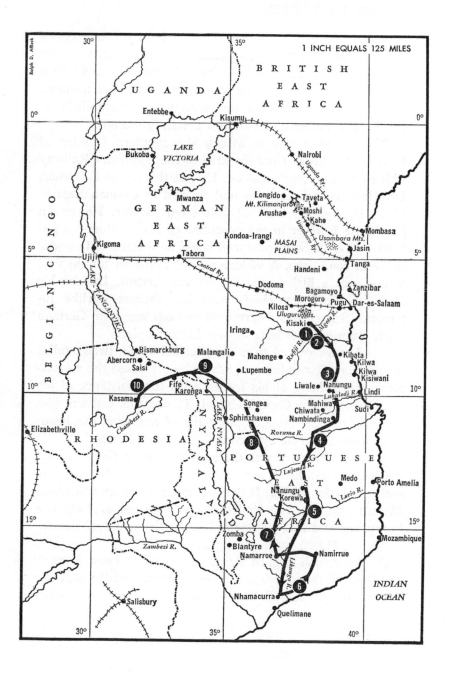

ness, it could be a very considerable thorn in the enemy's side. It was to provide a nuisance value; to keep as many Allied troops engaged against him as he possibly could, thus preventing them from being used in more decisive theaters. If the local authorities had any doubts as to the abilities of von Lettow-Vorbeck, von Lettow certainly did not.

His first plan was to attack the southern frontier of British East Africa from the area of the Usambara Railway which he had recently visited. He put this to the Governor, Dr. Heinrich Schnee, who had arrived in German East in 1912. Dr. Schnee was not interested in war. He was a passionate believer in the potential of his territory—a potential which he was convinced could be reached only under peaceful conditions. A visionary, but much on his dignity, Schnee was a little overawed by von Lettow. Despite his formidable military chief, with his obvious warlike intentions, Schnee was determined to keep war from German East. He would not hear of von Lettow's plan.

Von Lettow retired to a camp called Pugu, twelve miles inland from Dar-es-Salaam, where he organized the recruitment and training of his forces, with the assistance of his favorite officer, a Captain Tafel. It was this captain who first realized and taught "the value of rendering our headdress unrecognizable by means of grass and leaves."

At the outbreak of war the regular force in German East consisted of 216 Europeans and 2,540 askaris (*askari* is the arabic term for soldier. It came to mean a European-trained African soldier). The Police Force consisted of forty-five Europeans and 2,154 askaris. During the war 3,000 Europeans and 11,000 askaris were enrolled.

On the British side, in British East Africa (now Kenya) and Uganda, there were seventeen companies of the K.A.R.; African troops with British officers. No organized reserve to expand this force existed, but there were about 3,000 Europeans of military age in the two territories. Civilians were immediately enrolled to assist the regular force, in some cases to form their own units from local natives, in order to protect and patrol the frontier. One of the first to volunteer was Lord Delamere, who possessed exceptional knowledge and influence with the warlike tribe of the Masai. Lord Delamere was reputed to be "the mightiest lion hunter in Africa," and, not long before, he had entertained Theodore Roosevelt on his vast estate and provided him with some of the best sport on that sporting President's tour of Africa. He formed his own troop of "Masai Scouts." Another early volunteer was a Lieutenant Grey, brother of Sir Edward, a former British Foreign Secretary. He was wounded in one of the early frontier engagements and lost his left arm.

The war in East Africa began on the morning of August 8, 1914.

The British cruiser *Astraea* steamed within good range of Dar-es-Salaam and bombarded the town, aiming for the radio station. (German colonies relied on a network of radio stations for their communications to Europe and Berlin, unlike the British who were able to employ submarine cables.) A naval party from the *Astraea* also boarded and disabled two potential armed raiders in the harbor. All this met with no opposition from the townspeople, who had already, a little early perhaps, scuttled a survey ship and sunk a floating dock in the harbor entrance, thus rendering Dar-es-Salaam useless as a naval base for the remainder of the war—much to the fury of von Lettow.

A small party of Marines also went on shore and negotiated with the townspeople, who had the support of Gov-

ernor Schnee. A truce by which they would refrain from all
hostile acts during the war was signed. A German observer
of this episode wrote in his diary, "I saw a naval officer and
eighteen men land. I went up and found the Englishmen
speaking to a councilor at the customs office. While this was
going on the sailors were lolling about and some of them
occupied their time with carving their names—Thos. Cann,
Wm. Smith—on the government jetty as if already the
harbor belonged to them!" A similar truce was arranged
with the civil authorities at the port of Tanga, 150 miles
north of Dar-es-Salaam. A strong cable from the Admiralty
in London, however, demanded that the truces be repudiated.

It seemed that the observations of Mr. Norman King
about the citizens of Dar-es-Salaam had been correct.

Von Lettow had heard the naval guns while at Pugu and
marched down with the seven companies of askaris that were
by now available, only to find on arrival, with evident disappointment, that no British landing in force had been
made. Thenceforward relations between himself and Schnee
were strained.

Von Lettow was particularly handicapped by the fact that
his two main centers, the Central and Usambara Railways,
were not connected. The only practical way of getting from
one to the other at any speed was by sea; but British vessels
were patrolling the coast. Nevertheless, he decided to take
his force and join with other troops and volunteers in the
north, having finally got the agreement of Dr. Schnee to
launch an attack into British East Africa.

There were few who knew the route by land and none of
these could be found. No one, at this point, seemed anxious
to join in the business. However, the force set out and von
Lettow and one of his staff officers followed on bicycles part

of the way. Supplies were scarce and von Lettow learned on this march a lot about keeping his men on what they could scrounge out of the land and shoot on it. The heat was particularly severe and oppressive; the journey took two weeks.

Once in the north, von Lettow began organizing his command and preparing for an attack across the border.

One of the remarkable features about the whole East African campaign was the fact that it was fought, by both sides, for months on end without any reliable maps. On the march north von Lettow had already suffered from this. The deficiency lasted throughout the war. The German standard map of the colony was an imposing affair and at first sight appeared to be professional enough to inspire confidence. It was, in fact, far from accurate; moreover, large areas of the hinterland were entirely blank of detail. The makeshift British maps were even more inaccurate. Matters were further complicated by the various names for the same places in different native languages. Confused staff officers did not realize for some time that Makwele and Kwa Konje were the same place; or Kitovo and Kwa Mkomba. There were also many neighboring places with the same or similar names. Distances were hardly ever to be relied upon. Five miles on the map could mean anything from two to twenty-five miles. There were many unfounded suspicions of treachery because natives, supposedly loyal, insisted on giving distances of nearby villages totally different from those marked on the map. Because of the striking appearance of the German map, confusion was increased. For when it fell into British hands it was pounced on with sighs of relief—officers being convinced that at last they would be able to discover exactly how far they were from wherever they were meant to be heading. When British maps fell into German hands, similar or even worse chaos resulted. A note beside a name in a captured German casualty list read, "Lost and shot through using a British map."

Says the *British Official History*, "It is safe to say that no map used in this campaign could be relied upon as accurate by the standards prevailing in the European theater of war. To this must be added the fact that in the earlier stages many of the commanders engaged, not being trained regular soldiers, were unable to make the fullest use of such maps as there were."

The vulnerability of the British position in East Africa was quickly realized. With most of the K.A.R. away fighting remote tribes, the border with German East was practically unprotected. Both Nairobi and Mombasa, the chief towns, linked by the territory's only railway, were close to the border. Urgent help from India was called for, and on August 19 the first contingent of the Indian Expeditionary Force embarked from Karachi for East Africa. The I.E.F. was to be made up of various assorted units, none of which was particularly known for its fighting qualities. This rag-bag of a force consisted of the 29th Punjabis (only brought up to full strength at the last minute) and two battalions scratched together from various native states. There were also a mountain battery, R.A. (Royal Artillery), and a volunteer field battery from Calcutta. No one thought of the tasks that would confront this force and of the special nature of the fighting in which it was likely to be involved, when making up its composition. No one seems to have questioned whether an expanded force of locally recruited troops would not have been much better.

Meanwhile, many matters had to be considered as well as

the threat to the frontier, which border raids were already endangering. There was the matter of the lakes. As a line of communication these were vital. Lake Victoria seemed safely British, with only one German vessel there against a British flotilla of nine small steamers. Lake Nyasa also seemed safe. But on Lake Tanganyika the Germans were more prepared. The means of shipbuilding and ship-repairing had been set up. And owing to an extraordinary bit of foresight on the part of some German official, armor and guns had been brought from the coast at considerable expense and labor and were now being assembled on the lake. Already some Belgian craft on Lake Tanganyika had been attacked and destroyed, despite the anxious desire of the Belgian Congo authorities to remain neutral.

There was also the matter of the *Königsberg*. This German warship was the largest, fastest and most powerful in the area. She was newer (1907) than any British ship for hundreds of miles and she was also at least two and a half knots faster than her nearest rival. She had steamed out of Dar-es-Salaam on July 31 for a secret destination. For the next seven weeks she lurked about in East African waters, idling in the sun, discovering hiding places along the wild, inundated coastline—waiting to pounce like some fierce, savage greyhound. On September 23, she appeared off Zanzibar at 5:25 a.m. An armed British tug which stood guard at the harbor channel sighted her too late to raise an effective warning. The cruiser bore down on the port like a deadly shadow. After a few bursts of her powerful guns she sent her main rival, the British cruiser H.M.S. *Pegasus,* to the bottom and disappeared out to sea again almost before anyone had realized what had happened. There was not another British warship within a thousand miles. Where would the *Königsberg* strike next?

During August and September desultory fighting continued along the northern border of German East, as Colonel von Lettow-Vorbeck flexed his muscles and began to realize that he had the opportunity of taking Mombasa—which would be a really notable German overseas victory. Several parties made dashes for the railway, about forty miles from the border, in attempts to blow it up; if the British maps on which they had to rely had been more accurate they would probably have succeeded. The British post of Taveta, just over the border near Kilimanjaro, was occupied and later there was an engagement near Tsavo (famous for its man-eaters) when the newly-arrived Punjabis attempted to destroy some well-placed German maxim-gun posts by a bayonet charge. They suffered heavy casualties. But Mombasa was the main German target. The prestige value of its capture would be immense; more important as far as von Lettow was concerned, it was at that time the finest seaport on the coast. An attack was launched at the end of September, planned to coincide with the appearance of the *Königsberg* off the harbor. By now, however, the K.A.R. had all been recalled from the little wars near Italian Somaliland and in Uganda; the Indian reinforcements had arrived; the hurriedly mobilized volunteers had been organized into a fighting force of sorts; and, most important of all, the *Königsberg* failed to turn up. Six hundred German troops, with six machine guns, advanced into British territory along the coast and met a small British force of armed Arabs and motorcyclist volunteers, from Mombasa, twelve miles inside British territory. Women, children, rolling-stock and coin were evacuated inland from Mombasa. Slowly pushed back, the British force still managed to hold the German advance; two days later it was joined by a detachment of K.A.R. The Germans were unable to break the tiny British force com-

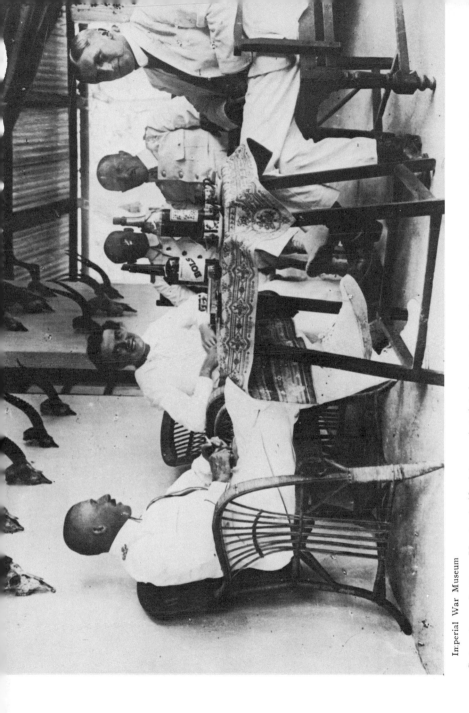

Colonel von Lettow-Vorbeck (2nd from right) being entertained on a plantation near Moshi, 1914.

Col. R. Meinertzhagen

German No. 13 Field Company parading at Kondoa-Irangi at the outbreak of war.

Col. R. Meinertzhagen

Issuing orders before the action at Tanga, November 4, 1914 (Sheppard—3rd from left; Malleson—center; Wapshare—4th from right; Aitken—right).

The German cruiser Königsberg *in East African waters, 1914.*

The Königsberg *at low tide, 1924.*

Col. R. Meinertzhagen

Indian troops embarking at Kisumu for Bukoba, June 20, 1915.

German military station.

Captain R. Meinertzhagen, British Chief of Intelligence, in Nairobi, 1915.

Col. R. Meinertzhagen

Major-General M. J. Tighe.

Col. R. Meinertzhagen

Major-General R. Wapshare.

Col. R. Meinertzhagen

Re-embarkation of Indian troops at Tanga, November 5, 1914.

The Mimi *(foreground) and the* Toutou *during trials on the Thames, 1915. (Spicer Simson in khaki.)*

The Mimi *and the* Toutou *on the way to Lake Tanganyika, 1915.*

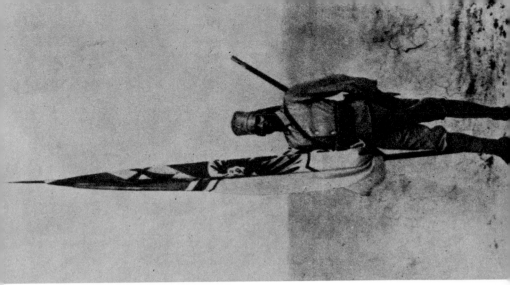

Col. R. Meinertzhagen

German askari holding the naval ensign of the König sberg.

Imperial War Museum

British camp at Morogoro, 1916. Uluguru Mountains in the background.

Hurst & Blackett, Ltd.

Von Lettow-Vorbeck (after the war). From My Reminiscences of East Africa *by P. von Lettow-Vorbeck.*

Ruckteschell-Trueb and Hurst & Blackett, Ltd.

"Askari. A halt" (a drawing by Lieutenant von Ruckteschell,
von Lettow's adjutant). From My Reminiscences of East
Africa.

Imperial War Museum

Suspension bridge constructed by Indian sappers in 1917 over a river in German East Africa.

Brigadier-General F. H. Cunliffe, in command of the Nigerian Brigade.

Nigerian Brigade on the march to Mahiwa, October, 1917.

Some of the Nigerian Brigade wounded after the Battle of Mahiwa, October, 1917.

Belgian troops returning to the Congo after the conquest of German East Africa, November, 1918.

manded by Lieutenant A. J. B. Wavell. The following week it was reinforced by Indians and the Germans were finally beaten back only twenty-five miles from Mombasa, after heavy losses on both sides. This was a remarkable and heartening little victory for the British, remembering that few of their troops had ever been under fire before and that they were opposed to well-trained, hardy, disciplined German askaris. Wrote one of the volunteers about Wavell's Arabs, "You must remember our troops were only hard little water-carriers." The German force was pushed back to its own side of the frontier.

Wavell was one of the many adventurers who lived in British East Africa. A cousin of A. P. Wavell, who became Field Marshal in the Second World War, he had been one of the very few to make the pilgrimage to Mecca successfully in disguise. He had left England in 1908 as a Zanzibari with a Turkish passport, and although suspected in Medina and Mecca, he had survived to tell the tale and to return to his farm outside Mombasa. He had recruited his force, known as "Wavell's Own," from Arabic-speaking natives. He was later killed in an ambush, with thirty of his Arabs, most gallantly firing after being wounded in the legs, until he was shot through the chest.

Fighting had been going on at other frontiers of German East. A German column had marched on Karonga, a small British township at the northern end of Lake Nyasa. The compound, about 100 yards square, was protected by a five-foot, loopholed wall. The town was successfully defended for three hours by only one officer, seventy African troops and police and eight civilians. A relief column arrived just in time, and after repeated bayonet charges the Germans retreated towards the border. The British force, said the Governor of Nyasaland, "was too exhausted to pursue." This action was typical of many other German raids across the frontier of German East. Nearly all of them were unsuccessful, but they left behind them a wake of crackling, burning villages, terrified natives and fear and anger among the whites.

So November began with no great gains for either side. But owing to the resolute defence of various British posts by courageous civilians and African soldiers, von Lettow was losing his chance; the only real chance he would ever have. For the British had prepared a makeshift force with surprising speed. And, despite the prowling *Königsberg*, a blockade was bound to come.

Von Lettow was inordinately proud of his capture of the unimportant post of Taveta, which he continued to hold. He had ordered a telephone link between the ex-British township and Moshi. The insulators were made from knocked-off bottle necks, fastened to branches of trees. The wire had been taken from the fences of plantations. Breakdowns were frequent; but von Lettow was delighted. He could, when the line worked, speak to his men who, after only a few weeks of war, were comfortably settled in British territory. But communication with the outside world was a different matter. In fact, since the outbreak of the war, German East Africa had been to all intents and purposes cut off. The British stations at Cairo and Khartoum no longer relayed messages. For the first few days it was possible to pick up wireless messages via Kamina in German Togoland, but soon these faded out. Under very favorable weather conditions they might get a snatch of a message direct from Germany. Apart from that they were isolated, and had no idea of what was happening in the war.

As for the British, they had staved off possible disaster at Mombasa. But German East was still there, controlled by the Kaiser's men, a worrying threat to Britain's East African colony. What was going to be done about it? An officer of the British staff remarked in a letter home, "The taking of German East Africa is obviously a much tougher proposition than the authorities ever anticipated."

Chapter 2
THE ACTION AT TANGA

At the same time as it had been decided to send a force from India to Mombasa, it had also been agreed that India should send a force to invade German East from the sea. And on August 17, Brigadier-General A. E. Aitken was designated to the command of this second expedition. Ten days later he was summoned to the cool offices and balconies of Simla—the seat of the administration in India during the hot season—where he met Mr. Norman King, late of Dar-es-Salaam. King talked to the General of some of the difficulties involved in invading a little-known coast. But the General was not greatly impressed with such pessimistic talk. His intelligence officer, a Captain R. Meinertzhagen, an Englishman who knew East Africa well, also counseled caution. Aitken replied, "The Indian Army will make short work of a lot of niggers."

ON TO KILIMANJARO

Meinertzhagen, the nephew of the famous British Socialist Beatrice Webb, was a violent, brainy and unusual soldier. A tall man with deep-set eyes and a military mustache, he later became a friend of T. E. Lawrence, who wrote of him, "A silent, laughing, masterful man; who took as blithe a pleasure in deceiving his enemy (or his friend) by some unscrupulous jest, as in scattering the brains of a cornered mob of Germans one by one with his African knobkerrie. His instincts were abetted by an immensely powerful body and a savage brain [*Seven Pillars of Wisdom*]."

Few people took much notice of General Aitken and the force which was being allotted to him to capture German East Africa. At Simla and Bombay men were grappling with the problems of despatching the main I.E.F. to Europe. In London few had thoughts of anything but the great German advance on Paris and the Battle of the Marne. With so many things on their minds the General Staff could hardly be expected to waste much time on the East Africa Expedition, or on its composition. The only certain thing was that the task was child's play and it would not require a crack force. After all, German rule was well known to be harsh. Was it likely that the native troops would, if pressed, fight on behalf of the Kaiser? Said a committee member in London, "I believe the smallest inducement would tend to make the whole of the German native troops desert to us, but in so doing they would probably murder all the officers' wives and children."

The two brigades that were chosen for this simple task were the 27th (Bangalore) Brigade, reputed to be the worst disciplined in the Indian Army, and the Imperial Service Brigade, which sounded somewhat more grandiloquent than it actually was, having been born there and then with a number of units from native states whose worth was unknown,

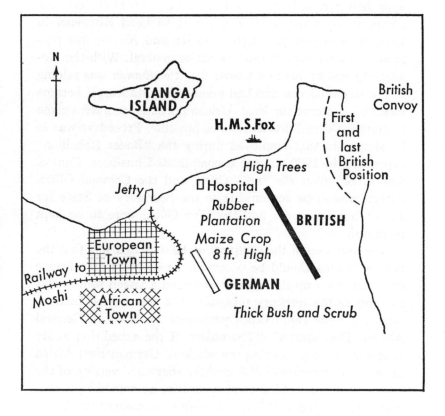

The Action at Tanga, November, 1914.

together with various odds and ends from southern India. Norman King labored at a pamphlet, *Field Notes on German East Africa,* to be issued to staff and other officers; the composition of the force was cabled to Lord Kitchener in London, who promptly agreed to it; and Aitken was promoted to a temporary rank of major-general. With the *Königsberg* still at large and news that the *Émden* was raiding in the Indian Ocean and had bombarded Madras, it became essential to secure the East African ports. Orders were given to start the expedition as soon as possible. Procedure was to be similar to that employed during the "Boxer Rebellion" expedition in 1900. It was a complicated business. Control was to be under the India Office and the Colonial Office. Aitken was to be responsible to the Secretary of State for India; but Kitchener and the War Office were to be kept informed.

The first step in the conquest of East Africa was that the port of Tanga should be occupied. From there an advance could be made up the railway and then a sweep southwards to conquer the territory probably in a few weeks. Instructions from the India Office were sent by letter to General Aitken. They started: "The object of the expedition under your command is to bring the whole of German East Africa under British authority." A slightly shortened version of the instructions was cabled to him, so that he should receive it before he left India. It is now known that, owing to a change in sentence between these two versions, it was not clear whether or not Aitken was *commanded* to take Tanga, or whether he could use his own judgment and possibly decide on a landing elsewhere. Aitken raised this matter with Simla and was told he "had better stick to" the plan to take Tanga.

The force was now assembling. Most of the units were strangers to each other and their new commanders. They came from far-flung parts of the subcontinent and spoke different languages and worshiped in different religions. None of them had experience in war, apart from a few who had fought on the North West Frontier and in Somaliland. Many of them were ill-trained; none had received training in bush warfare. Two of the battalions had not seen active service for more than a generation. Many units were still equipped with obsolete rifles and were only issued with Lee-Enfields (the sighting and mechanisms of which were quite different) immediately prior to embarkation; and one battalion not until after. Other battalions had no field telephones or pistols.

Said the senior staff officer to Aitken, after seeing the troops for the first time at Bombay, "This campaign will either be a walk-over or a tragedy." Meinertzhagen wrote of the troops in his diary, "They constitute the worst in India, and I tremble to think what may happen if we meet with serious opposition. The senior officers are nearer to fossils than active, energetic leaders."

One of the battalions was from the Regular British Army —the 2/Loyal North Lancashire Regiment. It was in the Bangalore Brigade, with three Indian infantry battalions. This was to be commanded by Brigadier-General R. Wapshare. The Imperial Service Brigade, under Brigadier-General M. J. Tighe, consisted of two full Indian battalions and two half battalions.

By the second week in October all were embarked and ready at Bombay (one of the Indian battalions was, in fact, on board sixteen days before sailing). But because of the general fear of the *Königsberg* it was decided that the expedition would have to join a convoy, protected by warships, bound for Europe. The ships lay out in Bombay harbor, with the troops inactive, cramped and bored. At last, the H.Q.

staff itself embarked (including the depressed Mr. King who everyone agreed must go along), and the same afternoon, October 16, 1914, at 5 p.m., the convoy of forty-six ships steamed away into the ocean. Fourteen of them carried the force of Major-General Aitken; 8,000 troops of "doubtful fighting quality" (*Official History*) who were about to attempt the conquest of a land nearly twice as large as Germany itself.

The force was to go first to Mombasa, the most southerly seaport in British East Africa, where a conference was to take place between Aitken and his staff and Brigadier-General J. M. Stewart, commanding the troops in British East Africa. The voyage lasted a fortnight. It was described by one of those on it as "a hell on crowded ships in tropical heat." Two days out of Bombay the greater number of ships departed for the Red Sea and Suez, leaving Aitken's little force chuffing across the basking ocean at an average speed of less than eight knots, accompanied by two ancient warships. Two days later the convoy was delayed twenty-four hours by having to turn back for three of the struggling transports which had been left behind. For the troops the voyage was a nightmare. The majority of the Indians had never seen the sea before. There was a gentle but persistent swell, which was just enough to provide misery-making seasickness. The ships were small and overcrowded. There was little deck space and exercise was difficult. Near the Equator the heat below decks became intense. Many of the Indians were not supplied with their customary food. To a man, they were dispirited, discouraged and wretched.

Meinertzhagen spent much of the voyage attempting to make Aitken face realities. He expressed the opinion that German colonial troops were the best in the world; that they knew the country and understood such warfare; that they were better even than the famous K.A.R. Aitken answered that "the German troops are ill-trained, ours are magnificent and bush or no bush I mean to thrash the Germans before Christmas."

At night on October 30, the headquarters ship steamed into Mombasa, leaving the rest of the convoy at sea, out of sight of land.

Aitken and two staff officers, including Meinertzhagen, went straight to Government House, where they met the Governor, General Stewart, Lieutenant-Colonel B. R. Graham, who commanded a battalion of K.A.R., and Captain F. W. Caulfield, R.N., of H.M.S. *Fox*, which was one of two ships to accompany the expedition to Tanga and provide fire-power. The Tanga project was discussed and also the part that the British East Africa force, under Stewart, was to play. It was decided the latter would attack at Longido, a post on a mountain northwest of Kilimanjaro, to coincide with the attack on Tanga—thus attacking the whole northern defence of German East at both flanks. "Information known about the enemy" was also discussed. This turned out to be very little. It seemed that the main German force was at Moshi and that the coastal districts were now not strongly held. Tanga itself was thought to be unoccupied by troops. The fact that, if this was so, troops could quickly be brought from Moshi to Tanga by rail had occurred to Meinertzhagen and he submitted a memorandum on the subject. This was ignored. Colonel Graham offered a contingent from his force, well versed in the techniques of bush fighting, to Aitken. He suggested they would be invaluable in the early stages, especially in covering the landings. Aitken, proud as well as confident, refused the offer without thanks. Meinertzhagen was "disquieted."

Information as to Tanga was scanty. It was known that it was approached by a tortuous channel through reefs and islands and was surrounded by much jungle and thick undergrowth. About the town were many coconut groves and avenues of mango trees and plantations. There was a quay, wooden buildings and a rail workshop. The European population was several hundreds. From two maps and an Admiralty chart a rough map (wildly inaccurate) had been prepared.

The subject of the civil administration of German East after its conquest was also discussed. Five British territories adjoined the area, and their respective claims were solemnly discussed and a memorandum on the subject sent off to London.

At the conference, Captain Caulfield casually dropped a shell as shattering to Aitken and his staff as any from his ship would have been. He told them of the truces which had been made at Dar-es-Salaam and Tanga in August by British naval commanders. When asked if the Admiralty had agreed to this, he said that it had not been informed. In fact, it had repudiated the truces and ordered local naval forces to formally enact this at both places as soon as possible. A ship had visited Dar-es-Salaam to carry this out; but it had not yet been done at Tanga. Caulfield insisted that before any attack on Tanga, the citizens must be notified of the repudiation of the truce. He was adamant. And though this formality would undoubtedly destroy all element of surprise, Aitken gave in. He agreed that it was essential to "play the game."

All the military at the conference were greatly depressed and returned to their ship.

They would have been even more depressed if they had realized that von Lettow was already fully aware of the little invasion preparing to attack Tanga. He read with interest allusions in the East African and Indian press, which were sent to him. Wireless messages from the Belgian Congo, mentioning the attack, were intercepted. Word had been passed among Africans from Mombasa and Nairobi. Many German residents in Mombasa were still free on parole. Von Lettow wrote, "It became more and more apparent that a hostile offensive was imminent." His trained eye realized that Tanga was the "obvious objective." And while the conference was taking place in Mombasa, he had arrived in Tanga and was discussing the defence of the place with civil authorities and driving around the countryside in a car.

Aitken and his staff officers rejoined the waiting transport ships.

Everything was settled. A suitable landing place was to be found by the *Fox*. The first landings were to be effected by the Imperial Service Brigade under Tighe, which was to occupy Tanga and take up a position inland. The other brigade was then to land at leisure and start the advance up the railway to Moshi. It was decided to go straight on and steam for Tanga, without disembarking the troops at Mombasa for a few days—for the sake of secrecy.

Such was the gist of the orders issued by General Aitken. The opening paragraph said, "From reliable information received it appears improbable that the enemy will actively oppose our landing."

No sooner had the convoy got up steam and moved off again than one of the two accompanying warships broke down, leaving only H.M.S. *Fox*. Even without the guns of the old cruiser, however, the force was still considered adequate. The convoy ploughed its slow way southward—just in sight of land. Columns of smoke were seen climbing from the shore; these may well have been signals of natives watching the progress of the ships. At a rendezvous fifteen miles east of Tanga, four tugs were met, towing lighters with 2,000 carriers from Zanzibar. No army could hope to advance in Africa without a force of carriers at least a quarter of its own strength, roads being practically nonexistent. Shortly afterward the convoy was halted, and H.M.S. *Fox* went alone into the channel outside Tanga harbor, flying a white flag. It was a misty early dawn that promised great heat later in the day.

Arriving in the harbor, with all crew at action stations, the *Fox* slipped up to near the quay and anchored. Captain Caulfield sent a message to the German District Commissioner to come on board. All guns were trained on the town, which appeared surprisingly quiet and empty of people. The commissioner was immediately brought on board. An intense and patriotic civil servant, he was at this time one of the few in German East who already admired the presumptuous von Lettow. Caulfield asked him to surrender the town; if he did not, it would likely be bombarded. He also insisted on information about mines in the approaches to the harbor.

Caulfield was particularly worried about the possibility of mines. Continual thinking about this in the preceding few days had made the matter an obsession with him. Meinertzhagen wrote in his diary, "He seemed nervous yet pompous, shifty-eyed and not at all inclined to help. It struck me that he was definitely afraid and was always referring to the safety of his blasted ship, ignoring the fact that it is his business to protect us even if he loses his ship."

Caulfield's voice sounded particularly tense when he mentioned the mines. The Commissioner was startled and, ow-

ing to a mistake of interpreting, he was led to believe that
he would be shot if he did not give the information. This, at
any rate, is the version given in the official account of the
episode. Despite this the Commissioner would give no information. He pointed out to the susceptible naval officer
that Tanga, an open town without defences, was not liable
to bombardment. As for the summons to surrender—he
would have to consult higher authority. He was given one
hour.

He thereupon left the ship, was rowed ashore, ran to his
office, sent off a telegram to von Lettow at Moshi and
warned the townspeople that a bombardment was imminent.
Having fulfilled his civil functions, he donned his uniform
as a lieutenant in the reserve, collected together all the local
police and reported for duty with the troops. The civil population fled the town into the plantations and the one company of troops, strengthened by the police, took up defensive
positions just outside the town. The whole process took less
than half an hour.

While all this was going on, the *Fox,* the dark green water
lapping on her old gray sides, idled in the harbor—waiting.
The scorching sun was rising in the clear, morning sky. The
German flag fluttered lazily in the breeze on top of the government buildings. Apart from the water and the distant
calls of tropical birds ashore, there was no sound. Tanga
appeared to be deserted.

Caulfield radioed General Aitken, explaining the situation,
and calling for minesweeping craft. After waiting an hour
and ten minutes, he sent a further message: "No surrender.
Rejoining convoy."

By midday the *Fox* had rejoined the convoy. Thus half a
day's warning of the pending attack had been given the Ger-

mans. Minesweeping now took place—with Captain Caulfield, having transferred himself to one of the sweepers, in personal charge.

Where to land? Aitken and Caulfield puzzled it out. The harbor looked dangerous. That silence was uncanny. And could not those houses along the front, apparently empty, in fact be full of waiting troops? Alternative landing places were considered, and at length a beach about a mile from the harbor was selected, on the far side of a headland, out of sight of the town.

General Aitken gave his final order: "The town of Tanga is to be seized tonight." The transports closed in towards the beach.

Meanwhile, many miles away, Colonel von Lettow-Vorbeck, with 1,000 of his best troops, was clattering down the Usambara Railway at full speed. The train of wagons full of tightly packed askaris, teeth and rifle barrels glistening, panted through rocky gorges towards the distant sea, the wailing siren of the engine blasting off at every bend.

Caulfield returned to the *Fox* about 3 p.m. and proceeded to rearrange the order of the convoy more to his liking; this resulted in further delay, as the transports, merchantmen with masters quite unpracticed at this kind of thing, got themselves into difficulties. At the same time the sweeping for mines was still going on. Over two hours later the landings had not begun.

On the *Fox,* someone thought he saw German troops near the shore and one round of 6-inch was fired into the bush (which was, it was later learned, deserted). The sun set in brilliant colors; darkness fell. Men clambered down into the lighters beside the transports.

The tugs towing the lighters received several sets of contradictory orders and it was not until 10 p.m. that the first troops were moved in toward the shore, with machine guns in the bows. Slowly dragging their way across the smooth water, bayonets shining in the bright moonlight, they approached the dark and sinister-looking tree-lined shore. Nearly 300 yards from the land the lighters, freed from the tugs, ran aground in shallow water. There they lay, clearly visible in the bright night, unable to go forward or to go back.

The water was just over waist-high—deep for heavily-laden men. It was not until an officer had waded to the shore and back safely that the Indian troops would follow him. Men waded ashore throughout the night, according to one observer "overcome with fear." Signal lamps flashed from shore to ship, and ship to shore. Brigadier-General Tighe and his staff landed. On board the headquarters ship General Aitken waited for the coming seizure of Tanga with impatience, giving opinion every now and again on what one of his staff officers called his "supreme contempt" for German native troops.

By dawn the majority of Tighe's force was on shore, although in an exhausted condition after little or no sleep, on top of nearly a month's seasickness and lack of exercise. A patrol was sent out through the bush and reached the edge of the town, from which it was fired upon by two machine guns. It promptly returned, but its report "was received with scepticism."

Everyone was surprised at the thickness of the bush, which consisted of palm trees, bramble and high grass (in some parts taller than a man). No further patrols had been sent out, and from all accounts the men were understandably jumpy, to say the least, suspecting the enemy behind every bush. The Lieutenant-Colonel of one of Tighe's three battalions—not having the faintest idea of the lie of the land or where the enemy, if enemy there were, was—took himself, his adjutant and another officer up a mound to gain a better view. All three were promptly shot down, one severely wounded and the other two killed.

Tighe's brigade of apprehensive Indians moved slowly forward, struggling with the dense undergrowth.

At this very moment, having now had twenty-four hours' warning of the attack, the first German train from Moshi arrived and stopped just outside Tanga, where the German askaris quickly jumped from the trucks and ran to take up positions. Almost immediately, they launched a counter-attack.

The first thing that happened was that the carriers from Zanzibar, bearing the machine guns of the 13th Rajputs, promptly dropped their loads in all directions and ran back towards the beach. The 13th Rajputs shortly followed, together with the rest of the brigade. As they ran, so they were shot down. The Germans, well versed in this kind of engagement, had snipers and machine gun observers in the trees. Because of the almost total lack of support, such isolated groups as did attempt to hold out, like that commanded by one brave officer, Captain B. E. A. Manson of the 61st Pioneers, were annihilated.

Fortunately, the Germans did not follow up the rout, and the firing, apart from an occasional shell sent by H.M.S. *Fox* into the deserted town, died down. By 10 a.m., the brigade was once again grouped around the beach, having lost a high percentage of its British officers (in one battalion, five out of twelve) and other ranks (a quarter in another). They saw, to their surprise, the last of the brigade still coming ashore— two companies having been marooned all night in a stranded lighter. One of the killed was an intelligence officer who was the only man in the force who had knowledge of Tanga and knew something of the layout of the town.

What had happened to the easy walk into Tanga? Tighe, somewhat shaken, reported to Aitken. It was decided that Wapshare's brigade would also disembark, and with the two brigades together, including the one all-British battalion, the surprising German resistance would soon be broken.

Wapshare's Bangalore Brigade landed throughout that afternoon, in a steady downpour of rain. Troops and stores began to clutter the approaches to the beaches and the shore itself. Late in the afternoon, General Aitken, not in the best of tempers, came ashore himself. All, including Aitken, were busy with the problem of disembarkation, which infuriatingly refused to be speeded up and which seemed to be continually beset with absurd but annoying difficulties.

So involved was everyone with these problems that no one thought of sending out patrols. No reconnaissance was carried out during the course of that hectic afternoon or the following evening. This was unfortunate. For, had they but known it, the British force could have walked into Tanga there and then—and unopposed. The Germans, fearing the guns of the *Fox* and the apparent size of the invading force, had evacuated their positions and retired up the railway line. Von Lettow himself had not yet arrived.

The confusion at the beachhead was made worse through the crowd of undisciplined carriers. A makeshift camp was set up for the night, men lying where they could, using crates and other stores to lie against. A sepoy fired his rifle by mistake, and the Indians of Tighe's brigade jumped up and rushed for the shore, and were only persuaded to return to their bivouacs with considerable difficulty. "Jolly fellows to go fighting Germans with," commented Meinertzhagen. The only two buildings in the encampment were taken over as a headquarters and a hospital.

Meinertzhagen made himself a bed out of some material from one of the houses. He wrote in his diary, "My mattress consists of the underclothing of the lady of the house, nice soft bits of lingerie, and for blankets I have a Union Jack and three German flags. My pillow is palm leaves stuffed into the corsets of a stout lady whose name I do not know."

The Indian Expeditionary Force to East Africa lay under the African sky and got what sleep it could. It had been November 3, 1914. Half a world away, at the Dardanelles, a historic British naval bombardment was warning the Turks of the danger of a landing—at a place called Gallipoli.

At sunset, the final landings were made. One of the battalions had been sent back to the transports before landing in the evening, and then returned, almost as soon as they had re-embarked, in the dawn. They had thus had little sleep or food before finally landing.

General Aitken now took personal control of the forthcoming engagement. His plan was based on conventional drill and tactics, taking no account of the exceptional conditions and ground on which the attack was to take place. The force was to advance in line with one flank next to the shore and the other inland. It was hoped that one flank would push inwards, thus outflanking the German defenders who were presumed to be lined up outside the town as on the previous day. The units which had been so shaken on that occasion were to be in support.

Owing to the difficulties of organization it was not until 12:10 p.m. that the order to advance was given. The troops delved again into the thick bush and dense rubber and sisal plantations. Movement was slow. Two hours later, after a few hundred yards had been covered, the enemy had not been engaged and it was still not possible to see any distance ahead. Gaps were appearing between units. The heat was intense, and men were fainting (although the North Lancashires were equipped with webbing, the Indian battalions still had old, leather equipment).

At 2:30, the Germans opened fire. They were, it seemed, in the positions expected. In fact, von Lettow had just arrived and brought the askaris, together with his reinforcements, back to the edge of the town. As the engagement started, the North Lancashires pushed on, outstripping the units on their flanks. Men fell all down the line. Half of the unfortunate 13th Rajputs turned and fled once more, taking most of a neighboring battalion with them. Said Meinertzhagen, "They were all jibbering like terrified monkeys and were clearly not for it at any price." They fired off their rifles in any direction, including at the backs of still advancing troops. The latter, imagining they were being attacked from the rear, also broke and bolted. "I had to use my boots and pistol to stop it." Meinertzhagen shot an Indian officer who drew his sword on him. Confusion and panic were winning the battle after only a few moments of action. Men lay face down in folds of the ground. Others prayed. Meinertzhagen ordered a sepoy, cowering with fear, to get up. He refused and threatened him with his rifle. "I shot the brute as he lay half-crazy with fear."

The unhappy truth was that the Indian troops were completely nonplused by a kind of warfare for which they were unprepared and in which they had received no training whatsoever. British officers, similarly inexperienced, did not know what else to do except to bully their men to blunder forward with them. How Aitken must have wished now he had accepted that offer of a detachment of the K.A.R. Von

Lettow's men seemed to know what they were doing. A survivor remarked, "They employed fire tactics certainly never taught in India."

Meanwhile some men of the North Lancashires and others had broken through and were actually in Tanga, despite the efforts of a German, Captain von Hammerstein, who stood and threw empty bottles at retreating askaris. Friend and foe were mixed up together, and, said von Lettow, "everyone was shouting at once in all sorts of languages." One group of North Lancashires reached the Kaiser Hotel and an officer climbed on the roof and brought down the German flag. But by this time many of the units had lost all their officers, and some of the leading companies still fighting had lost half their men. Not only were the well-placed machine guns proving deadly, but the askaris were also evidently well-practiced shots. Opposition in the town stiffened and fierce house to house fighting broke out as the Germans tried to winkle out those British who had succeeded in entering Tanga. The *Fox* was asked to give supporting fire, whereupon it promptly sent a shell into the town hospital and fired another into what remained of the British line, blowing the redoubtable Meinertzhagen into a palm tree. An artillery battery was still afloat, its guns held in position on deck by coal bags and its battery commander attempting to direct fire from a masthead. It was able to offer no useful support.

While all this was going on, a boatload of sailors from the *Fox* arrived at the quayside, in order to buy some food. They were lucky to get back alive, under heavy fire. Some of them were wounded and they only reached safety through three men swimming and pushing the boat along.

Receiving no reinforcements, the North Lancashires were forced to withdraw, and the German line once again soon closed. Says the *Official History*, "The rest of the attacking force, unhappily, was either dispersed among the thick vegetation or crowding back to the beaches." The carriers, among the first to flee, had been mistaken for German askaris breaking through because of their similar khaki dress and this caused further panic.

More alarm was caused by a sudden swarm of fierce and large bees. It was the native custom to hang their hives from the branches of trees. These had been riddled with bullets, and the bees, thoroughly enraged, were on the warpath. Both British and German units were plagued with the pests, but the belief that the swarm was some devilish trick of the Germans persisted for months in the North Lancashires. Several machine gun sections were put out of action after being attacked by these bees. A Conductor Preston, of the Signals, continued to take a message while being attacked by the bees and later had over 300 stings removed from his head. He was awarded the D.C.M. (Years after the war, von Lettow was asked by some British officers whether he had employed "trained bees" at Tanga. The legend was persistent. A postwar history book recorded that "canes and wires had been cunningly laid in the bush which, when trodden upon . . . drew the lids from hives of wild bees.")

Soon all that was left of the British line were a few officers fighting lonely, individual battles. The stampede at the beaches caused considerable firing by officers on their own troops. It was at this point that General Aitken, seeing with cruel suddenness his career and reputation crumbling all around him, himself charged into the fray with his staff. By his own example he urged the men to return to the fight. But it was useless. And according to a witness he was so distressed by the horrors of battle, groaning and screaming men, and officers being shot dead at his side, that his judgment and sense of control were, perhaps not unnaturally, further weakened.

Once again darkness fell. The British force was in total confusion. It had suffered 817 casualties out of 8,000 (Tighe had lost fifty per cent of his officers). If the Germans had counterattacked, there would have been a massacre. But they did not. Von Lettow, unaware of the demoralization of the British force and still apprehensive of the *Fox*'s guns, now firing more energetically into Tanga, decided to reassemble his force again outside the town.

As Aitken and his staff stood dejectedly in a small group, surveying the scene of confusion on the beach, they heard the clear notes of a German bugle sounding to them across the bush. This caused further panic, even among the headquarters staff. "My God, that's the Charge," shouted a staff officer.

Meinertzhagen, however, who had once lived in a German garrison town, knew that it was nothing of the sort. It was, in fact, the Retreat, and he told Aitken so. The bewildered General did not know what to believe. He told Meinerzthagen to go forward and see what had happened. With two volunteers of the North Lancashires, Meinertzhagen, bee-stung like nearly everyone else, approached the outskirts of the town unchallenged. Then he and his two men suddenly heard German being spoken only a few yards away. They fired at two or three shadowy figures, returned and reported that, apart from the one encounter, Tanga had been evacuated by the enemy. Meinertzhagen begged Aitken to allow him to collect as many troops as he could and claim the town. But Aitken refused. "He was tired out and seemed disgusted with the whole business. His one ambition seemed to be to get away." It was decided to re-embark. The attempt to conquer German East Africa by a landing at Tanga, so confidently undertaken, had been a disaster.

Some troops had been redisciplined and persuaded to ring the beachhead during the night. Another uneasy night was spent in the open.

While the British had been attempting to control their force, von Lettow had been wondering what was going on. He realized the British had suffered a setback. But he had no idea how severe this setback was. At his H.Q. in the bush behind the town he brooded on the problem of water, of which there was a shortage. The milk of young coconuts did something to quench the thirst, and so did bottles of wine and soda water. Hot sausages were brought to the troops by Tanga's leading butcher. During the evening von Lettow was just as unsure as to whether Tanga was held by the British as the British were as to whether he held it. So, "in order to satisfy myself quickly by personal observation," he hopped onto a bicycle and with two officers rode into Tanga. "I rode on through the empty streets of the town. It was completely deserted and the white houses reflected the brilliant rays of the moon into the streets which we traversed. We reached the harbor. Tanga was therefore clear of the enemy. A quarter of a mile out lay the [British] transports, a blaze of lights and full of noise. I much regretted that our artillery—we had two guns of 1873 pattern—was not yet up." Von Lettow then discarded his bicycle and walked down to near the beaches "where, right in front of us, lay an English cruiser [the *Fox*]." He had a further look round and then returned to the town. At this point he was suddenly fired on by a British patrol.

This was Meinertzhagen and his two men. If they had

killed von Lettow, the landing at Tanga might even have been worth while.

No thought of re-embarkation had entered the mind of any British staff officer until now, and consequently no plans had been prepared for it. When evacuation of the beachhead began the following morning it was a haphazard business. All units were disorganized, there were many men whose wounds were too serious to allow them to undergo the jogging and rough-handling necessary to get to the lighters, and the 2,000 chattering and undisciplined carriers further complicated matters.

It was decided that the more seriously wounded would have to be left behind, and so would most of the mass of stores which by this time had been landed. (One hundred and thirty seriously wounded were, in fact, left behind.) To facilitate the speed of re-embarking, machine guns were also to be discarded.

At dawn, the Germans began firing on the British ships with the two antiquated guns that von Lettow had now got into position. One of the transports was badly hit and set on fire. Owing to the swaying of the ships on the tide, the British were unable to reply.

The carriers were the first to leave, at 1 p.m. They were followed by the Indian troops. Owing to the haste with which everyone was anxious to get away, troops were put aboard any ship, not necessarily the ones in which they had arrived, and units were intermingled. Because of the tide, many had to wade up to their necks before they reached the lighters (in which some hundreds spent the following night before at last re-embarking). After a few random shots from a German patrol, according to the *Official History*, there was renewed panic and Indian troops "fled in chaos into the sea, swimming out to the boats, half swamping them and producing general confusion." Order was eventually restored "not without violence." Stores were destroyed, as far as time would allow—which was very little. The Kashmirs and the North Lancs. were the last to leave. The latter made a final appeal to be allowed to save their precious machine guns, but this was refused by General Wapshare. The last of the 7,200 men evacuated left the shore at 3:20 p.m.

Meanwhile, Meinertzhagen had been busy. "After a breakfast of warm water and rum drunk out of a bucket, and mighty good it was," he went to the field hospital and obtained a white sheet, which he made into a flag of truce. He then went off toward the German lines with a letter of apology from Aitken to von Lettow for having put a six-inch shell from the *Fox* into the hospital. On his way he came across the body of one of his best friends, killed the day before and horribly mutilated by German askaris.

In the German lines Meinertzhagen was welcomed with the greatest cordiality. Aitken's letter was sent off to von Lettow. The Germans were "kindness itself and gave me a most excellent breakfast which I sorely needed. There was a lengthy discussion over breakfast in the German officers' mess about the recent fighting, and all were fervent in their praise of the North Lancs. We discussed the fight freely as though it had been a football match. It seemed so odd that I should be having a meal today with people whom I was trying to kill yesterday. It made me wonder whether this really was war or whether we had all made a ghastly mistake. The German officers . . . treated this war as some new form of sport."

After breakfast Captain von Hammerstein arrived from von Lettow's H.Q. He acknowledged Aitken's note and Meinertzhagen then made his way back to the British lines. On the way a German askari fired at him from only a few paces range, not understanding the flag of truce. The bullet went through Meinertzhagen's helmet, touching his hair. "I went for him with my flag of truce and rammed him in the pit of the stomach which doubled him up. I then wrenched the rifle out of his hand and stuck him with his own bayonet. I was furious with him."

When he got back Meinertzhagen was told to go round all units and tell them that not only were machine guns to be left behind, but rifles and ammunition as well. He was horrified by this plan which would give "a wonderful Christmas present" to the enemy. He failed to pass on the order.

Recriminations and bitterness now afflicted the British force as it lay idling in the sun just off shore. Aitken and Wapshare were hardly able to talk together. They already had a deep mutual dislike and Aitken had been cold to Wapshare ever since leaving Bombay. Many of the officers on the *Fox* were also furious at the fiasco, especially at their own commander, Caulfield. "They were mutinous," Meinertzhagen wrote, "and spoke openly of wishing to shoot Caulfield." The officers said Caulfield could have brought the *Fox* closer in to Tanga and done much more damage, which was certainly true. Throughout, Caulfield was most reluctant to fire on the town. Meinertzhagen wrote in his diary, "Heavens alive, is this war or is it manoeuvres? From the bridge of the *Fox* we could see the steam of trains coming into the station and parties of German troops wandering about at less than a mile from us. I begged him to do something. No, he wouldn't. He said he did not wish to stir them up again. And all the time his ship was being sniped from the shore. Marvellous!"

A truce was now arranged so that troops on both sides could be sorted out and arrangements about the wounded could be made. Meinertzhagen, who seems to have been the only British officer to speak German, was sent off again to the German lines to reach an agreement about the British wounded left behind. This time he was rowed from the *Fox* in a small boat with a white flag. At the German hospital he again met von Hammerstein and concluded an agreement with him to remove the wounded the following day on the condition that none of them served again in the war. Meinertzhagen pointed out that "as regards the officers" they would have to be asked individually whether they would agree to this condition. Hammerstein showed some astonishment when he heard that the British were all back on board ship; and so did von Lettow when he heard of it. This was the first von Lettow knew of the re-embarkation. When he heard of Meinertzhagen's arrival and of the request for a truce, he was actually completing arrangements for a withdrawal of the German force inland, where defence would be easier and the climate less trying, and where they would be out of danger from the guns of the *Fox*. His astonishment at the British action was complete.

Meinertzhagen was liberally entertained with old brandy by the German doctor and they had a long discussion about the war in general. While they talked, he was able to see a party of snipers lying under some trees just outside the window, firing on the *Fox*. In one of the wards he visited an Indian Army major, who asked him what the chances were of getting away. He was under no parole or guard and Meinertzhagen told him to go ahead. The major thereupon got up, walked out of the hospital, down to the shore below, and persuaded a native to row him out to the *Fox*. Meinertz-

hagen watched it all from a window and once again he was
forced to muse that "it makes one wonder if this is really
war."

At 9 a.m. the following morning Meinertzhagen was back
again in Tanga. He and Hammerstein rode to the abandoned
beach on muleback, where he "officially handed over" the
British stores lying there. These included sixteen machine
guns, 455 rifles and 600,000 rounds of ammunition, telephones, clothing and equipment (von Lettow was delighted
and estimated that the clothing and equipment, especially
coats and blankets, "would meet all our requirements for
at least a year." Three newly raised companies were, in fact,
entirely equipped from this easily-won bounty.).

Inspecting the stores, Meinertzhagen was surprised when
he suddenly met the British Q.M.G. unprotected by any
flag of truce. "He was quietly making an inventory of our
abandoned stores." Hammerstein asked what he was doing
in the German lines, but Meinertzhagen explained that it
was a mistake and told the Q.M.G. to go back to the boats
immediately. No sooner had he gone than Hammerstein and
Meinertzhagen, hardly back at work, were astonished to
see a lighter of men of the North Lancs. approach from one
of the transports. The lighter stopped fifty yards from them
and the men jumped into the sea and bathed. Hammerstein
protested to Meinertzhagen that he would have to fire on
them, but the latter, after furious signals, got them to
return. "It was all very embarrassing," he wrote at the
time.

When the handing over of stores was finished the two
officers went off for breakfast—"good beer, ice, plenty of
eggs and cream and asparagus." They then bade farewell
to each other, exchanged addresses, promised to meet again,
and Hammerstein gave the British officer a photograph of

himself. After a talk with a young German officer, a bird enthusiast, about migration down the coast of East Africa, Meinertzhagen * left. But just before he stepped into his boat, Hammerstein took him aside and warned him that if the transports were not well away from Tanga shortly they would be fired on by the two antiquated field guns, although the Germans "had no wish to fire on unarmed transports."

Meinertzhagen reported this latest information to Aitken, on his return, and almost immediately all the ships up-anchored and steamed away for the open sea just as fast as they could go. For the past twenty-four hours, while the convoy had lain at anchor, the regimental officers and staff had been engaged in the delirious and humiliating task of trying to sort their force back into something resembling the units in which it had arrived.

Possibly the strangest feature of the unhappy procession was that leading it was the *Fox,* the ship provided by the Royal Navy to protect the convoy rather than lead it in escape. The last ship was, indeed, fired on from the shore, although without damage. Wrote Meinertzhagen, "I should imagine that such conduct on the part of the navy is unique." His annoyance may have been partly due to the fact that he was now suffering bad headaches through having been slung into the palm tree by the *Fox*'s shell.

The convoy anchored out of sight of land for the night, and the following morning proceeded up the coast toward Mombasa in melancholy procession, watched from the distant coast by the triumphant von Lettow on his bicycle.

The total casualties at Tanga were eventually reported

* Meinertzhagen was and is a great naturalist. Several species of birds and mammals are named for him.

as about an eighth of the force. Of these 359 were killed or died of wounds. The United Kingdom casualties, mostly North Lancs., were 127. No record was kept of the casualties among the wretched carriers. The total German casualties were 148. The engagement has long been considered the prime example of how not to go about an invasion from the sea. The British plan and execution were deficient in practically every respect. Intelligence was negligible. Enemy agents were active in Mombasa. The idea had been devised in London, where a proper appreciation of local difficulties was not made. The Indian troops were inexperienced and ill-trained. They were also lacking in discipline. Even the rudiments of jungle warfare had not been studied. The German native troops were grossly underrated. Most of the invading troops were sick and disgruntled before landing. The commanding general was working with a staff previously unknown to him. Neither Brigade Commander knew his officers. Ample warning was given to the enemy of the impending attack. Naval support was inadequate. When the capture of the town was at one point possible by merely walking into it, the opportunity was not taken.

From the German point of view, von Lettow had succeeded beyond even *his* confident hopes. About 1,000 of his men had beaten off 8,000. He had also received a windfall of valuable supplies. The victory brought a boost to the morale of his troops that would last for four years. And he himself had, in one stroke, gained a reputation of military invincibility that reverberated throughout East Africa. From now on the merchants and civil servants of Dar-es-Salaam were to treat him with respect, and many of them with adulation as well. It seemed that all was well for the great Fatherland. The last news to reach German East had been of the victorious invasion of France; no news of the reverse at the Marne had yet been received.

While Aitken had been launching his unsuccessful attempt on Tanga, the second half of the plan to invade German East Africa had been initiated at Longido in the north, as had been arranged at the conference at Mombasa.

It was believed that the German force here consisted of about 200 Germans and slightly more askaris (in fact, there were only eighty-six Germans, but nearly 600 askaris). The British force that marched across the bush to attack them was 1,500 strong. It was followed by 100 mules carrying water in tins. On the way, giraffes, ostriches and zebra cantered excitedly about, never far from the khaki column half-hidden in its own cloud of dust.

The Germans were strongly positioned on a ridge halfway up a mountain, and the approach to their lines was made at night. At dawn, the British column found itself in a thick mist about 1,500 feet above the plain. It was unable to go forward and unable to retire. German patrols stumbled on the confused British infantry, and when the mist lifted, a strong German force attacked and were only beaten off after a fierce counterattack by Punjabi troops. Unfortunately, however, the firing had stampeded the mule train, which careered back down the slopes, thus leaving the attacking force without water.

Isolated, without prospect of support and with no water under the hot sun, it was decided to withdraw under cover of darkness. Before dusk fell, two more German attacks had to be beaten off. The retreat was a difficult one owing to the nature of the ground. Men stumbled and fell. Some of the carriers panicked. At dawn of November 4, the whole force was back in camp after thirty-eight hours of continuous marching and fighting.

Unknown to the British, the Germans had been blessed by a singular piece of good fortune. For on the news of Aitken's force arriving at Tanga, von Lettow had ordered his Longido detachment to proceed to Moshi and Tanga. But by sheer chance signal communications between Moshi and Longido had broken down and so the orders for Longido were delayed. Had they been sent immediately, the British force would have been able to take the place almost unopposed and would then have had an entry to the whole Kilimanjaro area.

The news of the failure at Tanga was cabled by Aitken to London on November 5. It was a bitter shock to the Government who until then had displayed little interest in the East African campaign. The general situation was gloomy at that time. In Flanders there was desperate and inconclusive fighting at Ypres. In the Middle East, Turkey had joined the Central Powers. The German Admiral von Spee had won a victory at sea. It was felt that the time was not appropriate to inflict on the public the news of yet another reverse. And the Government was certainly glad of an excuse to hide the news of this total defeat, at any rate for the time being. East Africa was a long way off; few home troops were engaged there. It was decided that no mention of the Tanga action was to be permitted. Strict censorship was imposed. "Steps were taken" to prevent the news' spreading to India. The news of the reverse at Tanga did not reach the British public until later the following year.

Lord Kitchener was furious. Although he refused Aitken's

request that Indian regiments that had particularly disgraced themselves should be sent home, he discouraged decorations for any who had taken part in the affair.

The British convoy, returning from what the *Official History of the War* describes as "one of the most notable failures in British military history," reached Mombasa at midday on November 7.

While von Lettow's men were engaged in the unpleasant task of clearing the streets of Tanga, and the vicinity, of bodies ("the streets were literally strewn with dead and badly wounded; in unknown tongues they begged for help which, with the best will in the world, could not always be accorded at once") and burying the German officers in the shade of a great Buyu tree, the British too were encountering difficulties. The European customs officers at the port of Mombasa refused to allow Aitken's force to land its equipment or stores without paying duty of five per cent *ad valorem*. When Meinertzhagen threatened to arrest them, they sought the advice of the Governor.

The Tanga affair thus ended as it had started, in confusion bordering on the ridiculous.

Chapter 3

ON THE DEFENSIVE

Later in November, an alarmed committee met in London
to consider the implications of the Tanga fiasco. An exchange of huffy telegrams with Aitken ensued. While messages flashed to and fro, Aitken started on a long series of
heavy and cumbersome excuses. He said that there were
far more Germans engaged at Tanga than there actually
were. He said that the German force had been reinforced
by a detachment of reservists from Australia and China
(There were no such reinforcements). He urged that the
British should take on a defensive role in East Africa; in
no circumstances should he be asked to attack again—certainly not with troops that were unprepared to carry out his
orders. After a few days the telegram he longed for arrived
at Mombasa from the Secretary of State for India: "I am
reluctantly compelled to accept your opinion that we must

temporarily adopt a defensive role." The two Indian expeditionary forces, the Tanga force and the force that had already been stationed in British East Africa, were to become one. And the Cabinet decided, not surprisingly, that control of operations in East Africa was to be taken over by the War Office.

A few weeks later the unhappy Aitken was ordered home. His command was to be taken over by Wapshare, who was promoted to Major-General. When he received the message Aitken was in hospital with malaria. He sailed for England on December 17. Wretched years of disgrace and a bitter fight for his honor awaited him.

Wapshare was a kindly, somewhat nervous commander, who was generally popular. He was well known for his liking of physical comforts; a heavy man, fond of his food and with a dislike for taking unnecessary exercise. He was, however, according to Meinertzhagen, "no Napoleon . . . he is hopelessly ignorant on all subjects connected with his profession." He was known throughout Kenya as "Wappy." Meinertzhagen recorded an incident in his diary, shortly after "Wappy" took command. Wapshare got into a rickshaw, a normal form of transport in Mombasa. He sat down heavily, and the Swahili boy turned round and asked, "Wapi? Ju?" meaning "Where to? Up the hill?" The surprised Wapshare interpreted this as "Wappy, Jew?" He was incensed and walloped the boy with his swagger stick, who thereupon fled, tipping up the rickshaw as he did so and depositing Wappy in the street.

Efforts were now made to get the defence of British East Africa on a sounder footing. The staff moved up country to Nairobi, the administrative capital, and two military areas were set up: one from Nairobi and one from Mombasa, under Brigadier-Generals Stewart and Tighe respectively. All kinds of administrative problems had to be dealt with. The force was a polyglot one and British, Indian and Colonial services all differed in such matters as food, pay, allowances and munitions. Much of this jumble was never sorted out. (As late as 1917 two neighboring columns were differently rationed, equipped and maintained.) One Indian unit had to deal with paymasters in Britain, India, East Africa and South Africa. The railway line was hopelessly overworked, having to deal not only with the civilian population of B.E.A. and Uganda but with the troops as well.

From now, December, 1914, to February, 1916, the East Africa campaign was almost entirely on the defensive—against an enemy unable to launch a large-scale offensive. Many of the most important operations were naval: at sea, against the *Königsberg* and in blockades, and on the great lakes of Central Africa. But every day there were patrols probing the lines, especially by the Germans; every week minor clashes between patrols; every month a small engagement—usually when the British launched a minor attack to capture a stronghold a few miles behind the line. But for fifteen months von Lettow-Vorbeck was able to perfect his little army, to consider ways and means of maintaining his blockaded economy and to ponder on what was happening to that other German army of the Kaiser's, so far away.

Patrolling (on the Kenya-German East border) was an adventurous business. Wild animals, especially rhinos, were a common hazard. On one occasion a whole company of K.A.R. was completely routed by a charge of three rhinos. The patrol had to be abandoned. German raids on the railway were continually successful, despite the small detachment of K.A.R. and Indian troops down the line (the North Lancs. were scattered about all over the colony at supposedly strategic places). For a time a privately owned kennel of lion-hunting bloodhounds was used in attempts to follow the raiders. But the Germans were adept at quickly laying bombs to derail trains or damage bridges and then disappearing far into the bush on their return journey. They even had small bases from which they operated, inside the frontier. The wild borderland was little known to the British and it was a long time before all the water holes were discovered. The Indians, anyway, seemed to take little interest in guarding the railway.

In the beginning of 1915, a bitter little engagement took place at the unimportant fishing village of Jasin, which was right on the border. It seems that Wapshare, despite the new defensive role of the British force, had decided to have just one fling. At this battle von Lettow, walking in the open through heavy fire, got a bullet through his hat and another through his arm. This wound appears to have deterred him hardly at all and he refers to it only in passing in his memoirs. But his valuable aide, Hammerstein, died of wounds. A small British force of four companies was surrounded and hoisted the white flag; the remainder, after two months of sporadic fighting around the village, then returned behind the border from where they had come, most of them stricken with malaria. The British casualties were nearly 500. Says the *Official History,* "The morale of the British forces undoubtedly had again been shaken and they were not likely to be capable of passing to the offensive for some time to come."

Wapshare's effort to regain some small glory for the British force after the Tanga disgrace was rewarded with a reprimand from Lord Kitchener at the War Office. "You are entirely mistaken to suppose that offensive operations are necessary. The experience of Jasin shows that you are not well informed of the strength of the enemy . . . you should concentrate your forces and give up risky expeditions."

Von Lettow solved the problem of the German wounded at Jasin by organizing a convoy of rickshaw taxis from Tanga, a short way down the coast. When the grubby, bandaged, but victorious Germans from Jasin struggled back into Tanga they were received by the delirious citizens with tables loaded with free food and drink. And to heighten everyone's spirits still further, a wireless message had at last come from Berlin. It indicated that the Tanga news had just reached Germany; the Kaiser sent his personal congratulations.

The raids over the border by both sides continued. Stories were heard of a mounted band of German irregulars, and of a woman who accompanied them and inflicted indescribable cruelties on prisoners. The band was a conglomeration of several such groups; the woman was probably mythical. (An official British letter of complaint about her was sent to Lettow.) As 1915 advanced, demolitions on the railway became an almost nightly ritual. The number of undamaged locomotives steadily decreased. The troops guarding it became lower and lower in morale, chasing an efficient and speedy enemy. More and more men went down sick. It seemed that if the Germans attempted an invasion now, they might even succeed.

Wapshare had, since Jasin, become thoroughly apprehensive of the apparently invincible von Lettow. He believed him capable of anything. Meinertzhagen wrote, "He is terrified of him, and the mention of his name at Mess sends him off into a shivering fit of apprehension. It is not a pleasant sight." Later he wrote, "The chaotic state of affairs here is heartbreaking. No reserve, no discipline, lack of courage in leaders, thousands of unreliable troops and no offensive spirit. I wish to heaven I could get out of it all and fight in the trenches."

Such land action as there was during 1915 seldom occurred anywhere but along the Kenya frontier. But very occasional raids on forts and townships occurred along the Nyasaland and Rhodesian frontiers too. Early in 1915, matters in Nyasaland were complicated by a native rising unconnected with the war. It was put down by the local Europeans and by a column of K.A.R. who made a remarkable march to the affected area—eighty-six miles in forty-seven hours. The rising, instigated by a fanatical leader named John Chilembwe, caused considerable alarm and several Europeans were brutally murdered. A German lieutenant who had been wounded and captured some time before, and who was being held prisoner in a small township, organized the local defence and assumed military control of the station.

While their countrymen in Europe fought the bloodiest war ever known, in Africa Europeans were instinctively white men first—and German and British second. But John Chilembwe was part of something that, in the end, would swamp all their colonial dreams.

At this stage of the war it was not possible to send reinforcements from Europe to East Africa and many experts were convinced that stalemate was bound to result. For it seemed impossible to expand the local forces by any other means. Now that the first rush of patriotism and alarm that had accompanied the declaration of war were over, the white residents of British East Africa were showing singularly little willingness to join the local fighting forces. A public appeal for 500 additional troops received no response whatever.

Many Europeans returned to their farms. Some returned to England in order to volunteer for France, where it seemed there was more glory to be won than in an African colony. In a few months the East African Mounted Rifles dwindled from 500 to 250 men. The East African Regiment at one time got as low as forty total strength. Naturally enough, discipline and morale became slack.

Among the British and Indian troops, the inactivity, the frustration of trying to corner a fleeting, elusive enemy on the Uganda Railway, and the unhealthy climate combined to produce a general feeling of depression. Moslem troops had the added difficulty of contending with well-directed German propaganda. Despite incitements by the Aga Khan and the Sultan of Zanzibar, this got the better of some of them and desertions took place, and in one unit (a mounted unit of the K.A.R.) there was a mutiny.

In January, 1915, Lord Kitchener sent a mission to British East Africa to determine whether and how the local forces could be increased. It consisted of his elder brother, Colonel H. E. C. Kitchener, who had no experience of the colony, and Lord Cranworth, who had a great deal.

Kitchener did not create a good impression in B.E.A. He told everyone who would listen what he thought was wrong. He took copious notes of what everyone told him and said he would "inquire into it." On a visit to Zanzibar he bought a bag of cheap curios, including a walking stick made of rhino horn, three ebony elephants, two imitation ivory elephants' heads and some glass jewelry, for which he paid an exorbitant price. In a long report to the War Office he concluded that no large-scale increase in the local forces was possible. He dismissed the possibility of expanding the K.A.R., clearly having little opinion of their worth anyway.

Lord Cranworth, however, having especially consulted Colonel Graham of the K.A.R., submitted that "the main line to pursue must lie in the most rapid expansion possible of the existing King's African Rifles." Colonel Kitchener's views were broadly accepted in London. When the report was completed, its two contributors were obliged to stay in the colony and join the forces. Kitchener went off to command an obscure stretch of the Uganda Railway, and Cranworth joined Cole's Scouts, commanded by Berkeley Cole, a local resident and a friend of his. These were amateur soldiers, officered by aristocrats, ex-varsity sportsmen, black-sheep, and former cavalry officers who had turned settlers. They did some useful and dashing patrol work. Unfortunately, an officer attached to them sent a detailed report on their activities and attitudes to his own battalion H.Q., and this found its way back. He wrote, "There seems no sense of decency or deference among these officers." There was also an unsuccessful engagement in which the Scouts were involved, at about the same time, with heavier casualties than usual. A series of somewhat heated interviews between amateur Scouts and professional staff officers followed. Cole's Scouts were disbanded.

As newly-raised units were, however, the only possible source of reinforcement, Major-General Wapshare was informed that two new units would be joining his force, one a battalion of settlers from Rhodesia, and another raised in England called the Legion of Frontiersmen. A private offer to raise a battalion of Zulus and a battalion of Swazis was turned down. "Only *organized* troops can hope to carry through the invasion of German East Africa," it was said. A high percentage of such "organized" troops as were already in East Africa were sick with malaria and dysentery. Some had died. Others were dying. A large number would not be fit to march or fight for many months—possibly not until they left East Africa altogether.

The reluctance of British East Africa residents to join the force caused a good deal of bitterness between the colonials and the military. The latter looked on the former as cynical and too loath to leave their money-making farms and offices in order to serve their country; the former regarded the latter as slightly absurd and pompous soldiers, who had disgraced themselves at Tanga and were now making a lot of fuss about nothing—why carry the war to Africa anyway? The Germans across the border, they said, were nicely hemmed in and could not cause much harm. . . .

In Uganda the situation was much better. A local force, the Baganda Rifles, was formed during 1915 and did excellent work in the area west of Lake Victoria. The Governor there, Sir Frederick Jackson, placed all the resources of the protectorate at the disposal of the military.

One of the civil servants in Nairobi composed and circulated a song, "Steaming Down to Tanga," which ridiculed the troops. After a dinner, at which Wapshare and Sheppard were present, a lady got up and sang it:

> *Ping, ping, go the bullets,*
> *Crash explode the shells,*
> *Major-General worried,*
> *Thinks it just as well*
> *Not to move too rashly*
> *While he's in the dark.*
> *What's the strength opposing?*
> *Orders re-embark.*

Wappy was apoplectic.

The Governor of B.E.A., Sir Henry Belfield, allowed his officials to take leave in the ordinary way, despite the emergency. Throughout the early months of the war, according to Meinertzhagen, he spent practically all the time fishing at Mombasa, although his capital was at Nairobi. Wapshare asked him to return to Nairobi, but with no result.

Later in the year, when the Governor had at last taken up his post at Nairobi again, he was persuaded to see the Nairobi Defence Force, a volunteer defence unit. He suggested they go up to Government House, and this they duly did with band playing and flags flying. As they were marching up the drive they were met by the Governor in his car going in the opposite direction. They scattered in all directions, to make way, and then continued to the front of Government House, where they drew up to await his return. They waited in vain, for the Governor had taken train for the coast. This caused a local scandal; even the civilians thought it a bit highhanded.

On another occasion, a warship arrived at Mombasa commanded by Viscount Kelburn (now Lord Glasgow). An A.D.C. was sent off to meet the Viscount and invited him to Nairobi. A special train was then ordered for Kelburn and he was sent off on a shooting trip. The military were surprised to get a bill for the train from the Uganda Railway. The Governor insisted they should pay, as the game shot by Kelburn was used as meat for the troops. They refused.

As the year progressed, relations between military and civil authorities got worse. The soldiers seem to have had a lot to put up with, but the civilians, no doubt, were so little impressed with the efficiency of the army that they had difficulty in taking it seriously.

In April, 1915, the Legion of Frontiersmen left London for British East Africa. It is doubtful whether a more remarkable, romantic regiment has ever left Britain to fight abroad.

The casual observer would have noticed little difference that late night at number seven platform at Waterloo

Station. It was a commonplace sight to see a mass of khaki, awkward and ungainly in its kit, waving good-bye, smiling bravely and settling into the compartments. The men were, in fact, adventurers and soldiers of fortune collected from all over the world, officially dubbed the 25th (Service) Battalion, Royal Fusiliers (Frontiersmen). But in East Africa they were to be known as "The Old and Bold."

The battalion, 1,166 strong, had been recruited by a South African War veteran, Colonel D. P. Driscoll, D.S.O., who had raised and commanded the famous Driscoll Scouts in South Africa. After continual pestering and worrying of the War Office, he had been allowed to raise his force of Frontiersmen. The original intention had been to send it to France, but then someone, probably Driscoll himself, realized it would be better to send this motley collection of individualists to Africa, where they could do little harm and possibly a lot of good, than to the trenches, where their lack of discipline and training would make them more of a problem than a help. Driscoll, indeed, offered to invade and take German East Africa with his Frontiersmen alone.

The recruiting was partly done by advertisements in the newspapers and partly by word of mouth starting with Driscoll and his friends—some of them the original Legion of Frontiersmen that existed even before the war. Recruits included F. C. Selous, the famous naturalist, explorer and hunter, and friend of Theodore Roosevelt; W. N. Macmillan, an American millionaire of enormous physique (his sword belt was sixty-four inches in diameter); Cherry Kearton, the photographer who had specialized in photographing big game; famous hunters like George Outram and Martin Ryan; a millionaire from Park Lane; a royal servant from Buckingham Palace; a number of late members of the Foreign Legion; ex-cavalry officers from the 9th and 21st Lancers; a naval wireless operator; a circus clown; cowboys from Texas; several publicans; musicians from the dance band at the Empire Theatre in Leicester Square; London stock-brokers; a number of Merchant Navy officers; Americans from the United States Army; a lighthouse keeper from Scotland; Angus Buchanan, a naturalist who had been in the Canadian Arctic Circle when war broke out and had not heard of it for nearly three months—he made his way to join the Frontiersmen via Hudson Bay Fort and London; miners from Australia and the Congo; prospectors from Siam and the Malay States; pearl fishers; an opera singer; a pro-fessional strong man; an Irishman who had been sentenced to death by the President of Costa Rica; British officials and merchants from Hong Kong, Mexico, China and Egypt; a number of troopers from the North West Mounted Police; music-hall acrobats; a lion-tamer; and last, but by no means least, an ex-general of the Honduras Army, who became a sergeant in the Frontiersmen and built them a bomb-thrower.

The standard of experience of the unit was so high that it was decided to curtail all training until arrival in Africa. Most of the men had one or more war medals, including Matabele, Indian Frontier, Tongking, Madagascar, Senegal and others. But on arrival it was found that nearly half had never fired a British musketry course.

Senior N.C.O.s and warrant-officers of the Guards went with the battalion to Africa to help in the training. After the adventurous undertones of recruiting in London, and the leisurely voyage, the harsh discipline of the parade ground under the hot African sun must have come as an unpleasant shock to these volunteers, many of whom were past middle-age.

But they were soon welded into a formidable and invalu-able fighting unit, with playboys as privates and elephant poachers as majors, and until nearly the end of the campaign they saw as much hard fighting, went on as many relentless marches and experienced as much sickness and misery as any battalion in the war. One of them, Lieutenant Wilbur Dartnell, was to be awarded the posthumous Victoria Cross in a minor engagement shortly after the battalion's arrival. They had joined into a kind of Buffalo Bill army, for adventure and for patriotism. They were not to know that they were to get little but wretchedness. Before the war was over, most of them were to die in a remote, inhospitable country a long, long way from Tipperary.

Early in April, 1915, Major-General Wapshare was ordered to Mesopotamia, together with two regular signals sections. Popular as he was, many of his staff were not sure whether the signals were not a greater loss than Wappy. Tighe took over command. Brigadier-General W. Malleson was to take up Tighe's command at Mombasa, while Stewart remained in the west. Meinertzhagen wrote in his diary of Wapshare, "He was a great gentleman and a good friend, but his removal is for the public good, for he was a public danger."

On his way down to the coast to catch his ship, Wappy saw some ostriches from the window of the train, promptly pulled the communication cord, and, watched by the intrigued passengers, got out, lay down, and fired away at the ostriches, bagging two of them. Some of the passengers helped him drag the two birds into the goods van, where he spent the rest of the journey happily plucking them. The whole episode had taken place in a game reserve.

Compared to the florid and blimpish Wapshare, Tighe was a somewhat humorless man with a lean face and few words. He was, however, eager to fight.

On the way to Nairobi to take up his command, Tighe's train was ambushed and the line blown up. Bullets spattered into his carriage. The night was suddenly alight with rifle flashes from the surrounding bush. Tighe, infuriated by this cheeky raid, opened the door and dashed off into the night toward the flashes, waving his stick and swearing at the top of his voice. The ubiquitous Meinertzhagen was there too, firing away with what was, apparently, the only rifle on the train.

The Germans got away.

Tighe and Meinertzhagen guarded the train, full of chattering Africans, while the driver went up the line to wire for a breakdown gang.

Despite Tighe's ambitions to fight Germans, the campaign remained, on the whole, on the defensive. A telegram from the War Office told him to restrict himself to "protection of our own possessions." This was becoming increasingly difficult to do.

German infiltration over the border, with the purpose of wrecking the Uganda Railway, was becoming more and more evident and difficult to stop. Toward the end of April, a bridge was blown up, which put the line out of action for several days. More units were dispersed all down the line, but it was impossible to guard every mile of a railway 400 miles long. Moreover, the Indian troops were as disinterested as ever. One of their posts was stampeded by two rhinos, whereupon its garrison fled. A sentry at another was attacked and eaten by a lion. The Indians, to a man, desired only to get home. There were increasing numbers of self-inflicted wounds. Only the North Lancs. had much success in guarding the railway, and they were suffering more severely than any other unit from sickness. Throughout the campaign the battalion was always seriously depleted. At one time or another every single member of the battalion was in hospital, but because they were the only regular British unit, they were continually being called on for minor engagements.

Matters were not helped by the extraordinary order given to some posts that sentries were to carry a rifle at night but not during the day. Moving patrols up and down the line was not a simple business. Each Indian sepoy of the 13th Rajputs, for instance, was entitled to five porters—two to carry his ammunition, one his rifle and equipment, and another two to carry his blanket, rations and personal articles.

Led by expert scouts and stalkers the German-officered askaris continued to do much as they pleased.

Various precautions were taken by the Railway. Trains were restricted to fifteen miles an hour. Engines were preceded by a truck loaded with sand. Von Lettow's men countered this with a detonating device that was set to go off after a certain number of wheels had passed over the track. When this was discovered, the engines were put behind still more trucks.

To the south, German East Africa was bordered by Rhodesia and Nyasaland, as well as Portuguese and Belgian territory. Here sporadic fighting, far away from the problems of Generals Wapshare and Tighe, had continued throughout 1915. This was a wild and desolate part of the continent, which was still hardly settled. Local administration had existed for less than a generation and the white population was small and widely scattered.

Because of the communications advantage that an early control of Lake Nyasa gave them, the Germans were in a better position than the British. It was soon realized that the garrison at Abercorn, the chief British settlement of the area, would not be enough to control the border and stop a possible thrust into Rhodesia, which would bring great prestige to von Lettow.

A post known as Saisi was therefore established near the border. A fort was built in a knoll of solid rock (by breaking the rock with fires and then suddenly cooling with water —owing to the shortage of explosives). An outer ring of trenches and a thorn-fence barricade completed the defences. A garrison of Northern Rhodesian police and Belgian troops, about 400 altogether, was established.

Before long (July, 1915) a German force, 300 strong with two field guns, arrived to take Saisi. They dug in opposite the British emplacements and for three days bombarded the little fort. On the third day the garrison began to run short of food and also suffered agonies from thirst, there being no well.

The following day the sound of distant firing told the defenders that a relief column (of Belgian troops) was on the way. But only a small detachment, thirty-four, managed to get through to Saisi. The siege went on. Three days later, when there was hardly any food or water left, there was a German summons to surrender. It was refused. But by a mistake the British officers who went out to meet the white flag were fired on. A formal apology was received later the same day from the German Commander. As one who fought in German East said, "The conduct of the war in this sector was courteous."

During all this time, and until February, 1916, the telegraph line between Abercorn, in Rhodesia, and Bismarckburg, in German East, remained in operation. The two postmasters kept it open by a daily test signal.

After a failure to charge and storm the barricade and

trenches, the German force withdrew from Saisi. His Majesty's Government shortly conveyed its appreciation to the Belgian Government for the heroism of the Belgians both in defending Saisi and in attempting to break the siege. A long and confused series of meetings between British and Belgian authorities produced no very satisfying agreement about cooperation in the war in East Africa. There was a good deal of suspicion on both sides, especially on the British, where it was suspected that if the Belgians conquered any of German East Africa during the war, they would stick to it afterwards. It was not, therefore, until the end of the year, when the Belgians had returned to their own territory to fight the Germans on their own Congo border, that it was thought wise to appoint an overall commander in the southern area. Brigadier-General E. Northey sailed for Capetown on December 4. He had commanded a battalion from Mons to Ypres, where he had been wounded. A forceful, efficient soldier, he was coming to a very different kind of war.

The campaign in German South-West Africa, where the South Africans under Botha had routed the small German force, had now drawn to a close. But a column of Germans and rebel Boers who had joined them tried to break their way out across Bechuanaland and Rhodesia, to join von Lettow in German East. With a large train of wagons and animals, they made their way via the Victoria Falls, pursued by Union troops. After a long chase, much of it through desert where no white man had been before, the German column reached Portuguese East Africa, where they were interned.

A Major R. Gordon achieved notoriety through chasing, and eventually catching, a smaller party of Germans on a similar mission. For eight days he traced them across the wilderness, covering 135 miles, rounded them up and brought them back 400 miles to Livingstone.

Meinertzhagen spent the year of 1915 perfecting his intelligence service. When he had arrived in Mombasa, German residents there were at large. He had asked Belfield to arrest and detain them all, only to receive the reply "I consider nothing less than extreme urgency would warrant course proposed." Before Meinertzhagen's arrival, the Game Department had carried out the duties of Intelligence. Now he got down to organizing a small but quite remarkable service of his own. Almost immediately he caught two native agents in Mombasa. They were tried and shot.

He made frequent expeditions, often alone, in the border area, examining German posts. On one occasion he was looking down at a German camp from a hilltop and writing notes, when he suddenly saw a German officer slowly walking towards him. It was typical of both Meinertzhagen and the German East campaign that both men discovered they were, unaccountably, unarmed. Meinertzhagen wrote in his diary that night, "Should I remain hidden and let him pass, should I spring out on him and strangle him or should I just say, 'How do you do?' To hide would have been almost impossible, for he would have been bound to have seen me. To murder him in cold blood seemed unnatural. So when he was not more than a few feet from me, I jumped up and said, *'Guten Tag.'* " They had a short, stilted conversation and then ran off in opposite directions.

Soon Meinertzhagen had some 100 agents operating from Mombasa, who were frequently in and out of German territory, mainly in the coastal area (by 1916 his agents and scouts had increased to 3,000). Farther inland he collected about twenty Europeans, mainly hunters, at least one of whom became a legend, to report on border movements. But his best agents were Swahilis, who went in and out of German East on errands for what Meinertzhagen described as his DPM system—Dirty Paper Method. His agents visited the German officers' latrines and the material they brought back, though filthy, was invaluable to the H.Q. staff. Messages, troop movements, notes on coding, and the signature of every senior German officer in the area were all obtained in this way. A DPM organization was set up with "post offices" under European supervision, and the method was an unqualified success.

Meinertzhagen's most dangerous opposite number was an educated Arab who had supplied the Germans with a quantity of accurate information. He was especially active in the sabotage of the Uganda Railway. Meinertzhagen attempted in vain to counter his activities and then tried a simple ruse. He sent him a letter thanking him for his useful information as a double agent and enclosing a sum of money in German currency. He gave the letter to his worst agent and told him to deliver it to the man at his home in Mwanza on Lake Victoria. The messenger was caught by the Germans, his letter discovered and Meinertzhagen's rival convicted and shot.

Meinertzhagen rendered about eighty miles of the railway secure from attack by littering the edge of a pool, the only well for miles, with dead animals and labeling it "Poisoned." The first German patrol to visit it afterwards turned back without drinking and one man died of thirst on the return journey. No further German raiding parties went near the area.

Another one of his efforts was to introduce counterfeit currency into German East. Also, a German naval lieutenant who had deserted was disguised by him with "red

ON TO KILIMANJARO

beard and dark glasses" and put in a prisoner-of-war camp
at Nairobi, from where he passed on information gained
from fellow prisoners.

Meinertzhagen was bitterly insulted when the *Nairobi
Leader* printed an article attributing the failure at Tanga to
the fact that the British intelligence officer there had been a
German Jew. Meinertzhagen, not a man to turn the other
cheek (his name is of Danish origin), had the editor arrested
and his paper closed down for seven days.

Meanwhile, Tighe was finding his new responsibilities a
heavy burden. Not least among them was Brigadier-General
Malleson. A stream of complaints from the coast reached
Tighe and eventually he sent for Malleson. On arrival in
Nairobi, Malleson decided to go off for a lion shoot. Twenty-
four hours later he had not returned and there was some
alarm. It turned out that he had found no lions, but had
spent the night at a farm where there was a farmer's pretty
daughter, and having told his driver to return to Nairobi,
he had been forced to return on muleback. In all the excitement about this disappearance, Tighe forgot about his inter-
view with Malleson.

Another incident that tried Tighe's patience was the affair
of the ex-general in the Honduras Army, now in the Frontiersmen, and the giant gun. This imposing machine, constructed in the Uganda Railway workshops, was at last completed. After being inspected by a number of ordnance and
artillery officers, it was taken to a plain near Nairobi for
testing in front of Tighe. A canvas target was fixed nearly a
mile away. The gun was loaded with a dynamite bomb, with
great care, and the inventor then stood back and pulled the
lanyard. There was a tremendous explosion, a cloud of
smoke and a blast of gassy fumes—but very little gun.

ORT

ON THE DEFENSIVE

About this time Tighe took to drinking heavily. He became quickly irritable and jumpy, and, apparently, was at the bottle most of the day. Said Meinertzhagen, "A good soldier, as straight as a die and drinking himself to death in the middle of the greatest war in history. Sad."

Meinertzhagen's last reconnaissance of the year was made just before Christmas. His small party sighted four tents with some men lounging around bush fires. They waited till dusk, and then rushed the camp with bayonets fixed. The askaris were bayoneted before they could reach their arms. Meinertzhagen himself rushed into the officer's tent, where he found a surprised German sitting on a camp bed. Laid out on a table before him was a Christmas dinner.

The officer groped under his pillow and Meinertzhagen was forced to shoot him. The total haul was nine prisoners and fifteen killed. Meinertzhagen and his second-in-command, of course, sat down and ate the Christmas dinner.

During 1915, von Lettow was strengthening his economy and his forces, as well as doing his best to destroy the Uganda Railway. One of his greatest problems was transport, as his two railways served only a portion of his territory. For instance, rice, brought from the Lake Victoria district, took at least a month to reach Moshi, and each carrier himself needed two pounds of food a day, the maximum load of a carrier being fifty-five pounds. A track connecting the Central Railway to the Usambara Railway was made and on it at least 8,000 carriers were continuously employed, split up into large groups covering stages. Doctors traveled up and down the road doing what they could for the dysentery and typhoid of the carriers. Bridges were built, including one of stone and concrete.

Von Lettow had some trouble in getting men to go out on

raids on the Uganda Railway. The land was mostly desert or sparse shrub and many died of thirst or starvation after getting lost. Von Lettow himself records cases of Europeans' being reduced to drinking urine on these sorties.

But, on the whole, morale was high despite the blockade by sea and the lack of communication with Europe. Von Lettow strove to encourage an atmosphere of comradeship among all his officers and N.C.O.s. Decorations and awards were practically unknown. Rank was less important than normal in German forces. Every able man was recruited, including some aged over sixty.

Von Lettow was not only an excellent administrator and a commander of talent but also a brilliant improviser. His successful attempts to keep his economy going were reminiscent, as he himself later wrote, "of the industry of the Swiss Family Robinson." He was able to harness the latent, almost religious industriousness that seems to surge from Germans when they are beset with industrial and economic ambition. Old books giving information about the forgotten techniques of hand spinning and weaving were hunted up. Soon spinning wheels and looms were constructed, and women at home and in private workshops were spinning by hand—just in time, as the stocks of cotton clothing in merchant's shops had completely dried up (there were, of course, cotton fields in plenty). After several trials the root of a local tree was found to produce the best dye, of a brownish-yellow color similar to khaki. Rubber gathered by planters was vulcanized with sulphur and makeshift tires for automobiles and bicycles were produced (tires were also made by tapping rubber trees directly on to rope). A group of planters successfully produced a motor fuel of sorts, similar to benzene, from coconut. Candles and soap were made out of tallow and wax. Bags for grain and other produce were made from palm leaves. Cigars and cigarettes were manufactured from locally-grown tobacco. Rum and whisky (ninety-two per cent proof) were distilled. Nearly all the factories and plantations in the colony were commandeered by von Lettow to help with the war effort.

Boots were made from the skins of cattle and game; tanning materials from mangroves. The first boots turned out in quantity this way came from Tanga. The Kilimanjaro farms specialized in butter and cheeses. Sausages and smoked meats came from Wilhelmstal. Cloth, rope and string were being made at Morogoro from pineapple and sisal. Fruit juices and jam were produced at Dar-es-Salaam.

Most important of all, quinine, so vital to the health of the Europeans and almost exhausted, was produced by a biological institute at Usambara, from wood bark. Those who were dosed with this draft known as "Lettow-schnapps" swore that its effects were worse than malaria itself. The government institute, which before the war had been looked on by the settlers as expensive and useless, also produced castor oil, chocolate, rubber hose, and even rubber nipples for babies' feeding bottles, an article of which there had been a grave shortage. All these articles, and others including small-arms ammunition, mines and artillery shells, had never been produced in German East before, and many of them are not produced in Tanganyika today.

In a speech to the population of Dar-es-Salaam on the Kaiser's birthday, Governor Schnee was proudly able to declare, "The enemy cannot crush us economically. We get all we require from the country. We find all our food supplies, materials and necessities in our German East Africa. The value of our colony shines forth in this war. I think that many of those who have known the country for years doubted if we should succeed in meeting the requirements of the population, white as well as colored. There is, however, I may say, an unexpected wealth in this country, such as we had never imagined in the past, and we find we have an adequate supply, even of such things as previously we have thought it necessary to import."

A maximum number of units, totaling sixty companies, was eventually obtained. Von Lettow considered it unwise to expand any further than this, owing to the limited number of Europeans available as officers. But the establishment of the companies was raised from 160 to 200. The total strength by the end of 1915 was 2,998 Europeans and 11,300 askaris.

Von Lettow realized that eventually an invasion of his territory would come, and that it would come from the north. As early as August, 1915, he started evacuating his precious stores and materials to the south. A railway line for this purpose was built as far south as Handeni, at the rate of one and a quarter miles a day.

Von Lettow was perturbed to discover one day that these activities were being watched from the skies by airplane pilots newly arrived from South Africa. The natives, who believed the machines to be a new god, were even more surprised when one was shot down and a white man walked out of it.

From the summer of 1915, von Lettow waited for the big attack from the north that he knew must come. In June he occupied himself by directing the dismantling of a telegraph line in British territory, and putting it up again in his own.

At home in the U.K., the public had only the haziest idea of what was going on in East Africa. The war in France and Flanders was developing in a way that few had suspected, and most people were only concerned with the heavy casualties at the Battle of Loos. Long after Tanga, there was official reticence about events in East Africa. Letters home were strictly censored. But in a speech to the Victoria League in London, the Colonial Secretary, Lewis Harcourt, spoke of the thrills and romance of the war in East Africa: "A campaign of gallantly captured posts, of conquest and reverse. Sometimes a cruiser—more often a launch or a lighter—capturing a defended port or taking an enemy ship; bridges blown up or repaired, railways attacked or defended, wireless stations destroyed or erected, the tentacles of an impregnable and united Empire stretching out in its embrace, unhasting, unyielding, the personification of the power of the seas."

If anybody wanted to know what was happening in East Africa—now he knew.

On November 22, 1915, General Sir Horace Smith-Dorrien, late of the Western Front (where he had been criticized for his objections to mounting frontal attacks against well-prepared enemy positions), was appointed to command a new expedition against German East Africa—and most of his army was to come from South Africa. It had been decided, far away in Whitehall, on a bleak winter's day, that East Africa was to become an important theater of war.

The days of Wappy and Tighe were over. The campaign in East Africa began a new phase.

Chapter 4

NAVAL OPERATIONS

For more than half of 1915, the *Königsberg* had remained the prime concern of the naval forces off the East African coast. Until it was sunk, no Allied vessel in the Indian Ocean could be safe and no blockade of German East could be secure.

Late in 1914, a German hospital ship, which was flying the Red Cross flag but was not painted white, was stopped and boarded by the British cruiser H.M.S. *Chatham*. Papers on board this ship revealed that coal had been sent up the Rufiji River in lighters. There seemed only one reason why so much coal was needed in this sparsely populated area. Captured charts showed that the Rufiji was navigable to the *Königsberg* for several miles upstream. And there, in the complicated channels of that river, the *Königsberg* was found at last. With her were a collier and three small steamboats. But not only could the *Chatham* not get at her, owing to the lack of detailed charts of the labyrinthine delta and the possibility of mines—she could not even sight her. For it was learned from natives that the German cruiser lay more than ten miles upstream, in a creek of one of the many tributary channels. It was protected by entrenched troops on the surrounding banks, and by shore batteries.

Tighe himself was sent down the coast by the India Office, in the *Fox,* in order to investigate the situation. He decided that a landing near the *Königsberg* would be most inadvisable. The lessons of Tanga had been well learned.

A block ship was sunk at the mouth of the channel up which the *Königsberg* lay and a number of ships were left to watch her lest she should escape down some other channel, while the remainder, including the *Fox,* went off to bombard Dar-es-Salaam, an operation which, says the *Official History,* was "of no military value." The Governor's palace was destroyed, a fact later regretted by the occupying British.

A cable was sent by the Admiralty to Jan Christian Smuts: "Have you an elephant hunter Pretorious in South Africa? We would like him for a special mission." Pretorious was found and put ashore near the Rufiji, where he had hunted and farmed before the war. By this time seaplanes had arrived on the scene and they were able to determine the precise position of the German ship—surrounded by tall jungle which was by now almost growing over her. The hovering planes soon discovered two more channels through which the *Königsberg* could break out and reach the sea. This brought further alarm and Royal Navy ships scurried back up the coast to the delta. But there, for over six months, the *Königsberg* stayed.

At last, on July 4, 1915, a determined effort was made to do away with this menace once and for all. Two waddling river monitors, H.M.S. *Mersey* and *Severn* (flat-bottomed craft armed with three 6″ guns and two 4.7″ howitzers) made a slow and dangerous journey from England and finally attacked the German ship with high-angle fire. Their guns were directed by an observer in an airplane, an early example of such warfare. After six hours of almost ceaseless barrage, they set the *Königsberg* on fire. With two cruisers and three sweepers sounding and sweeping the channel, they closed up to the German vessel.

On July 11, the *Königsberg* was finally put out of action. But her guns (including ten 4.1-inch) were salvaged and were destined to turn up again and again during the campaign, much to the discomfort of the British, as they were larger than anything in the British artillery. For the transport of these heavy guns, trolleys found on a nearby plantation were used. The crew also survived and provided valuable European reinforcements to von Lettow's land forces; while some of them even managed after twelve months to return to Germany by way of dhows to Arabia and then by land to Turkey. The cruiser itself lay battered and useless, abandoned and half sunk. Her rusting sides were rubbed by tick-infested hippopotami, while crocodiles slithered across her decks and fish swam in and out of her open ports.

German East Africa was bounded in large sections of its inland frontiers by the three great African lakes, Victoria Nyanza, Tanganyika, and Nyasa. Of these, Tanganyika was, in the early part of the war, almost entirely under German control. On the other two the balance was more in favor of the British.

During the first fortnight of the war, services on Lake Victoria had continued between German and British ports as usual—"it being considered essential to maintain the usual communications." But soon the lake boats were armed, and they prowled about, in the vast open reaches or close to the shores, in this enormous lake almost the size of the Irish Sea. Three of the British flotilla on the lake were armed with a 12-pdr. gun each and manned by naval ratings. They were authorized to fly the White Ensign and the officers were all either Royal Naval Reserve or granted temporary commissions. They attacked similarly-armed German craft, visited hostile posts and sought out the German dumps of wood fuel that were known to line the banks. (This was done with more than usual care after a decoded German wireless message revealed that it was proposed to dump tempting piles of logs around the shores, with one of each pile hollowed out and filled with dynamite—an intention worthy of Meinertzhagen himself.) There was some consternation when one of the armed British steamers, the *Sybil*, struck a rock. Her captain unwisely reported that she had been mined. The officer who was sent up to make a report wired to headquarters, "*Sybil* holed by an unexplosive mine laid by the Almighty, 4000 B.C." The captain was relieved of his ship.

In June, 1915, Tighe decided on the ambitious project of attacking, from the lake, one of the two main towns on the German shore of Lake Victoria—Bukoba (the other being Mwanza). After some haggling, the War Office gave its assent. There were 1,500 German troops in the vicinity of Bukoba and Tighe detailed some of the best troops in B.E.A., including the 25th Royal Fusiliers (Frontiersmen) and the North Lancs., to take part in the engagement. A total of 1,600 men, with two guns and twelve machine guns, under the command of Brigadier-General Stewart, embarked on a fleet of six steamers. About twenty hours later they arrived in the evening off the shore north of Bukoba—with lights ablaze.

The Germans immediately realized what was happening and sent up a rocket and flares for aid from nearby troops. At this, the little British fleet turned about and steamed back into the night. It returned four and a half hours later and the Fusiliers were the first to disembark. Heavy fighting followed and the British were unable to make much progress against an enemy located outside the town in rocky land, and with well-placed machine guns. There was no reserve, and the General commanding was in the firing line.

Firing ceased at night and the troops bivouacked where they found themselves. There was no food; it had, apparently, been forgotten.

The following day the town was taken. After a number of light skirmishes the outnumbered Germans retreated to the bush. The wireless station and fort were destroyed under Stewart's supervision. What followed is either not mentioned or glossed over in most accounts of the affair. According to Meinertzhagen, however, Driscoll asked Stewart for permission to loot the town, and this was granted. He wrote in his diary, "I went into the town where the Fusiliers were looting hard. All semblance of discipline had gone, drunkenness was rife and women were being violated. Men were threatening their officers. . . . British soldiers in fancy dress wearing German officers' full-dress helments, African porters clothed in European ladies' undergarments, savages smoking Henry Clay cigars and drinking champagne from the bottle and throwing stones at a huge picture of the Kaiser."

The *Official History* has a different version. It says that the "Sack of Bukoba" occurred after the force had re-embarked, when the town was at the mercy of "the surrounding tribes."

As the ships steamed away at sundown across the vast

lake, there was some chaos and confusion aboard. The units were all hopelessly mixed, as they had re-embarked in haphazard order. Some of the officers were drunk, some of the men loaded down with loot. A captured German gun slipped from a lighter into the lake. Thus ended this sordid little affair which was of very little military value in the war against Germany, but which provided an outlet for the frustrations of soldiers who had been too long on the defensive against an enterprising enemy.

On Lake Nyasa there was less activity. In August, 1914, a British boat sent a shell into a German lake-craft, whereupon the astounded German captain, unaware of the outbreak of war, rowed out to the British vessel to find out the reason for this outrageous behavior and to his great irritation found himself a prisoner-of-war. This episode resulted in an indignant article in a Cologne newspaper entitled "War Without Chivalry." In March, 1915, a detachment from the *Fox,* of three officers and six ratings, with five 6-pdr. guns, reached the lake overland and took charge of the British boats there. A raid was made on the German lake township of Sphinxhaven. A landing party made a hectic bayonet charge, whereupon the garrison fled into the bush. The only dangerous ship in the harbor was disabled, the force re-embarked and British command of Lake Nyasa was assured.

Lake Tanganyika, 450 miles long, the largest freshwater lake in the world, had been discovered, like the other great African lakes, only fifty-four years before the First World War. But already, in a generation, a number of small ports and townships had been built on its shores, and steamers regularly plied between them on strict timetables.

At the outbreak of war the Germans were able to collect

about 400 riflemen in their lakeside settlements, and these they turned into a kind of detachment of marines. They also armed a number of vessels, including the *Hedwig von Wissmann* and the *Kingani* (which had been brought by rail from Dar-es-Salaam), and constructed a raft on which they mounted a 3.5-inch naval gun—with which they bombarded a number of Belgian stations on the opposite shore. After a small land-sea battle with the Belgians, the German marine force captured a number of machine guns and, equally useful, nearly 100 miles of telegraph wire. The township of Kigoma was fortified and developed, according to the *Official History*, into "a base for naval warfare."

There were no armed British craft on the lake (the British shore, in Northern Rhodesia, was less than 100 miles), and the Belgians had failed in their attempts to curb German influence on it. It seemed that German command of the lake, so important to them for quick transportation from north to south in the western area of their colony, was indisputable. And thus their left flank in the event of any advance from British East Africa, was well protected.

In April, 1915, however, a big-game hunter who knew the lake well, J. R. Lee, suggested to the Admiralty that the German domination of Lake Tanganyika *could* be broken. His ambitious idea, instead of becoming lost and forgotten in a file, was not only studied at the Admiralty but agreed and acted upon. For this, the Admiralty deserved a great deal of credit—for Lee's ambitious plan seemed at first sight to be a practical impossibility.

His suggestion was that a naval detachment, with light motorboats, should be taken out to South Africa and then transported overland to Tanganyika. The force of the plan was strengthened by a similar proposal arriving shortly afterward from the War Office. It was decided that an attempt was to be made, and the enterprise was entrusted to Lieutenant-Commander G. Spicer Simson, R.N., who had experience of Africa in Gambia and elsewhere. The Admiralty decided to treat the lake as a sea within "the sphere of British naval power."

The expedition numbered twenty-eight Britons, of whom Spicer Simson was the only regular naval officer (there were a number of R.N.V.R. officers). The boats were two fast motor-launches of almost four and a half tons, and forty feet long. Christened *Mimi* and *Toutou*, they had been built for a foreign government, but were commandeered. Because of their small size, there was some difficulty in arming them. One 3-pdr. was mounted on each. No one was quite sure what would happen when these guns were fired, or whether the boats would be navigable under the recoil.

On June 12, 1915, the boats and men left England and reached the Cape at the beginning of the following month. Their journey was made with the utmost secrecy. From the Cape, they had 8,000 miles to go.

The first stage was taken by rail, via Bulawayo and Livingstone, and then on to the railhead just north of Elizabethville in the Belgian Congo, for this was as far as that magnificent Victorian dream, the Cape to Cairo Railway, had managed to stretch. The craft then had to be taken across 150 miles of jungle to the Lualaba River, where they could be taken down to another railhead that would finally transport them to the lake. Cutting across this strip of jungle was a range of mountains 6,000 feet high. At first, this journey was divided into fifty-mile stages, a depot being arranged at the end of each stage where supplies could be collected and a pause made for recuperation. The boats were carried on specially-made wagons, pulled by traction-engines. Much of the way was untracked and unknown; makeshift bridges had to be constructed across ravines and torrents. Progress was slow, as a path had to be hacked and cleared before the advancing engines. When the hills were reached, it was found that even two engines were not enough to pull the boats up the gradient. A team of oxen and every man pulling, together with the engines, also failed. The heat was intense.

It seemed that the gallant attempt to reach the lake had come to an end. But Spicer Simson was a man of resources. He arranged a pulley system, with the aid of tree trunks, by which the oxen pulled downhill, and the boats were gradually raised up the slope. Six weeks after leaving Cape Town, the plateau was reached. But then came the way down— which if anything was more difficult still. There was a continual risk of losing the craft altogether down the steep mountain-sides and precipices.

When at last the flat was reached again, both men and beasts were utterly exhausted. But somehow they had to move on as quickly as they could, for they were now suffering from a serious lack of water— not only for the men, but for the machines as well. When once more they were almost giving up, civilization was reached again; and a light railway took them the fifteen miles down to the Lualaba River.

There followed 400 miles of river transport, in which the boats were towed with corks fastened beneath them to protect them from sandbanks and rapids. Several times they grounded. At one stage they had to be carried on a flat-bottomed steamer. The railhead to Lake Tanganyika was reached on October 22, and the 150-mile journey to the lake was made on railway wagons.

During all this time, natives in the pay of the Germans had been watching the progress of the expedition from river shores and from thick jungle. It was with some amazement that von Lettow's staff realized what the British were doing and it seems that they did not take so mad a scheme very seriously.

Nearly five months after they left England, *Mimi* and *Toutou* arrived at Lake Tanganyika. The boats were hidden until a breakwater and a launching pad, made of rails running into the water, had been constructed. This took the best part of two months. They were launched, stocked up with ammunition and otherwise prepared, and by Christmas Eve all was finished. The Royal Navy had arrived on Lake Tanganyika, right in the heart of the continent of Africa.

Christmas Day, 1915, was a day of rest for the expedition, but during a makeshift service the following day an alarm was sounded. The German ship *Kingani,* fifty-three tons, was steaming right past the British base. Both the British launches were hurriedly manned and gave chase. The Germans were evidently surprised at the sight of two swift British craft on the lake. Suddenly, they realized that the rumors they had heard were true. After a ten-minute fight, the *Kingani* surrendered, there being only one survivor. The *Mimi* had made twelve hits out of thirteen rounds fired. By the time she was towed into the British base the *Kingani* was almost sinking, but she was patched up and made into a third British warship—the H.M.S. *Fifi*—and fitted with a 12-pdr. gun which, when fired, according to Spicer Simson, stopped the boat in its tracks even when going at full speed. This capture was just as well, as the *Toutou* was shortly afterwards sent to the bottom in a violent storm.

In February, the *Hedwig von Wissmann,* three times the size of the *Kingani,* was sighted by the two British boats. A running fight of thirty miles followed, lasting about three hours. The *Fifi* was left behind, but the *Mimi* hung on to the German boat, firing all the time, and keeping her to a zigzag course. The *Hedwig* was sunk after several hits. This episode is the basis of C. S. Forester's story, *The African Queen*.

The largest German boat, the *Graf von Götzen*, 850 tons, declined to come out in the open lake. Eventually found scuttled in the German base, she was raised after the war and, having been carefully greased by the Germans, was still in good condition and continued in service throughout the 1920s and 1930s. The only other dangerous craft on the lake was in a state of reconstruction after a checkered career. This was the tug *Adjutant*. After the outbreak of war she had slipped out of Dar-es-Salaam, breaking the blockade, but eventually fell into British hands. Turned into a gunboat, she took part in the operations in the Rufiji delta, until she had run ashore on one of the mudbanks of that river. Captured with her crew, she was taken to pieces by the Germans and transported bit by bit up the railway to Kigoma and Lake Tanganyika, where during the latter part of 1915 the Germans were having some difficulty in reassembling her.

Despite all chances to the contrary, therefore, Tanganyika was now entirely under Allied control, whereas nine months before the German command of this lake seemed undisputable. Spicer Simson was promoted and awarded the D.S.O. Three of the other twenty-eight members of the expedition were awarded the D.S.C., and twelve the D.S.M. It is doubtful if any other "sideshow" of the war had a greater effect on one campaign. For, from now on, 450 miles of von Lettow's border was in perpetual danger.

As early in the war as December, 1914, a blockade of the German East African coast had been suggested by the Colonial Secretary, but it was not until the following spring that the Admiralty had enough ships on the scene to attempt to enforce one. And for a time, of course, the problem of what to do about the *Königsberg* in the Rufiji occupied most naval minds in East Africa.

On April 14, 1915, H.M.S. *Hyacinth* had chased a cargo ship, the *Rubens,* into a bay just north of Tanga and had there, it was supposed, destroyed her by shell fire.

Later that year, however, some startling news was received at British G.H.Q. about the *Rubens.* A Mr. Munro, who had been interned by the Germans at Bukoba on the outbreak of war, had been released during the raid on that town. He said that the *Rubens* had not been fully destroyed and her cargo, which consisted of munitions from Germany, had all been salvaged. His story was at first received with some scorn. But his information linked with that received by Intelligence from other sources.

The story was perfectly true. The ship, known to the British as the *Rubens* and to the Germans as the *Kronborg* had successfully run the blockade after an adventurous voyage from Wilhelmshaven. Disguised as a Danish vessel called the *Kronborg,* the superstructure had even been changed to make the resemblance more complete (the real *Kronborg* was believed to be on a voyage from Sweden to La Plata at the time). A wireless was secretly installed. Danish-speaking Germans (mostly South Jutlanders) were asked to volunteer for the crew, but none knew where they were heading or the nature of their cargo until they were some days out at sea. They were given false names and false Danish papers. They were even paid Danish seamen's wages. The only two persons in German East who knew of the voyage were von Lettow and the commander of the *Königsberg;* somehow they had been informed. The *Kronborg*'s cargo was coal for the *Königsberg* and arms, ammunition and supplies for von Lettow's army.

The ship made its way across the North Sea, into the

Atlantic between the Shetlands and the Orkneys, well west of Ireland and Portugal, then down the west coast of Africa, round the Cape of Good Hope, to the north of Madagascar, and then straight in on a fast run northwest to Tanga.

When the ship was finally cornered by H.M.S. *Hyacinth,* it lowered its Danish flag and steamed full ahead for the shore. The *Hyacinth*'s shells hit her and she appeared to be on fire; a party from the British cruiser was sent out to make sure that the destruction was complete. They reported that this was so and the *Hyacinth* steamed off. The German crew had swum ashore and watched their ship burning.

What had happened was that the German commander had ordered the decks soaked in petrol, the burning of which deceived the British. The salvaging of the munitions, most of it in perfect order, although some of the ammunition had suffered from the sea-water and needed attention, took many weeks. There were enough Mauser rifles (1,800) to re-equip a large part of the German force, which had previously been making do with rifles of 1871 pattern. There were four and a half million rounds of small-arms ammunition, several small field-guns and machine guns, and ammunition for them and for the *Königsberg*'s guns, and such general supplies as 200 tents and materials for telegraph services and medical supplies. Meinertzhagen claims that one of his agents saw the whole episode and actually assisted in the salvage operations. The *Kronborg* lay in Mansa Bay till 1940 and may well be there to this day.

The crew were also of much use to von Lettow, especially the skills of the engineers and wireless operators. This sudden windfall was of incalculable value to von Lettow-Vorbeck in continuing the war in German East. It also raised morale. As he said, "It proved that communication between ourselves and home still existed." It was a tenuous communication and it might be the last they would ever have, but it was something that meant more than mere arms and supplies to the Europeans.

But on the whole it seemed that the days of von Lettow's impudent stand against the British Empire were soon to be over. He had lost the priceless cover that command of Lake Tanganyika had given him in the west. He had been contained in the north, and also in the south, where General Northey was taking up his command. And to the east there was only the Indian Ocean and the unlikely chance that the German High Command, with all its other problems, would send out another blockade-runner.

In South Africa, a new army, bigger and better equipped than anything seen before in East Africa, was already embarking for Mombasa. Whereas, at the outbreak of war, there had been anxiety as to the loyalty of the Union, now there was little. The rebellion of 1914 had been crushed. It seemed that the Boers really had decided to throw in their lot with Britain once and for all. Most of the rebel leaders were either dead or in prison. It had not been pleasant; but perhaps the nightmare of South Africa was over at last. Under Botha, the South Africans had swept the Germans out of Southwest Africa. Now they were about to do the same thing in East Africa.

On the Western Front, the Battle of Loos had been a disaster. In the Mediterranean the attack at Gallipoli was at a standstill; it seemed that total evacuation would have to come. In "Mespot" (Mesopotamia) an uncertain advance was in preparation against Baghdad. On the Eastern Front the Russians were giving way under heavy Austro-German pressure.

Perhaps in East Africa, a theater that had received little

attention from either those who directed the war or the public, a great Allied victory could be won. Men began to look towards Africa with increasing hope, desperation and interest. In London a set of rooms in a private house in Park Lane was offered to Smith-Dorrien; it became a center of much bustle and activity in connection with the new campaign. The staff of the Commander-in-Chief met together and discussed the problems shortly to face them. Mostly cavalry officers, they began, with some glee, a search for "men with a taste for adventure." These were to be Special Service officers, who were to take on special duties. A Bulgarian missionary, called Verbi, visited the offices in Park Lane and persuaded the cavalry officers there that he was just the man they were looking for. Verbi claimed enormous "influence over the wild men amongst whom he had lived and worked." The War Office refused to give him a commission at first—Bulgaria was, after all, at war with Britain and therefore he was an enemy alien—but they gave way in the end. Another of the Special Service officers had just returned from service with the Cossacks in the Carpathians; another was a gold-miner from Madagascar. They, and five more, remained with the force for some years—but little is on record of their activities, if any. Major Josiah Wedgwood, member of an influential family, also called at Park Lane. He was anxious to see what armored cars could do in the bush, and was enthusiastically given his head. (It turned out that armored cars could do practically nothing in the bush.)

General Smith-Dorrien, who had been hurrying on his way to B.E.A. to take command of the new army and Tighe's assorted force, had fallen ill on the very first day of the voyage and developed pneumonia. By the time of his arrival in South Africa he had recovered, although not fully, and he began making arrangements for his campaign. This was something to which he was looking forward with considerable pleasure, as his talents had gone almost completely wasted—as had General Allenby's—on the Western Front. He was known to be not only a man of independent mind, but a thoughtful and intelligent commander.

He became more ill and instead of resting tried to continue with his work. Ill-health forced him to resign and he returned to England. If he had been able to continue with his appointment and had conducted the war in German East, it is interesting to speculate what success he might have had. Perhaps he would have made the same mistakes as the commander now designated to take his place—Lieutenant-General Jan C. Smuts. Perhaps not.

Smuts's appointment caused considerable confusion and dismay to the staff being assembled for Smith-Dorrien in B.E.A. They found that they were mostly to be replaced by Smuts's henchmen, all "amateur" soldiers. Among them there was some bitterness at the choice of Smuts, who was not considered a "professional" soldier. But everyone had to agree that the choice was helping recruitment in South Africa tremendously.

By now it was known to von Lettow, via his "bush telegraph," that a South African army was coming to do battle with him. The long-expected invasion from British East Africa was about to begin. He did not, however, view this prospect with any dismay. He wrote, "It was important to encourage the enemy in this intention, in that the South Africans should really come, and in the greatest strength possible, and thus be diverted from other and more important theaters of war. With the greatest energy, therefore, we continued our enterprises against the Uganda Railway."

One of the main German posts, for the railway operations, was at Salaita, near Taveta, and before the arrival of the great General from South Africa, Tighe and Malleson decided to launch a large-scale attack on this camp. Aerial reconnaissance suggested that the total German force was about 300 and that they were in trenches north of a hill. About 6,000 troops were put into the attack, one of the largest so far in the campaign. It seemed it could not possibly fail. Many of the troops were newly-arrived South Africans who spoke of the German askaris as "only native troops."

The attack failed. The German trenches were on the hill, the others being dummies especially constructed to confuse aerial reconnaissance. There were about 1,250 German troops at Salaita, not 300. After a bayonet charge by the askaris, the British force retired—the South Africans suffering 138 casualties.

The overwrought Tighe was at the quayside to welcome Smuts as he arrived at Mombasa on February 19, 1916. The short, well-knit figure, red beard streaked with gray beneath his red-banded staff cap, stepped quickly and purposefully down the gangplank. No one was more delighted to see him than Tighe.

Within days, confidence had returned in British East Africa.

Chapter 5

ON TO KILIMANJARO

In a year and a half of war nothing like Smuts's first few days in British East Africa had been seen before. He went straight to Nairobi. In less than twenty-four hours he was off on a personal reconnaissance, close to the enemy lines in the Longido area, having ignored the various receptions and functions in his honor that the local citizens had prepared. Going from hilltop to hilltop, across scrub country where neither beasts nor men lived, in energy-sapping heat, he scanned German camps and emplacements through his battered, favorite field glasses.

On his fifth day he called London, telling the War Office that an immediate offensive, before the rains came in March, was essential. Its object would be to clear the Germans from their important area around the foothills of Kilimanjaro, the great snow-capped mountain that has haunted so many African travelers. Permission was given and preparations were immediately put under way. Smuts's plan was the same, in all except detail, as one already prepared by Tighe and much of the organization necessary had been made before his arrival.

Troops in the western area and around Nairobi were to be a new 1st Division, roughly corresponding to the previous Nairobi area force under Brigadier-General Stewart. Stewart was still to be in command of the division. The second division was to be made up of those troops who had been largely concerned with the defence of the railway; it roughly corresponded to the old Mombasa area force. The 2nd Division was to be commanded by Tighe. Malleson, who had commanded the Mombasa area, was given the command of a brigade in the 2nd Division. The two divisions consisted of Indian, British, East African, K.A.R., and South African and Rhodesian reinforcements. Most of these were men who had already seen long and frustrating months in B.E.A.

The bulk of the South African Expeditionary Force, under Brigadier-General J. L. van Deventer, also made up a division. Recruiting in the Union, under the urgings of Botha, had gone much better than expected. Recruiting had opened in November and by March there were two infantry brigades, a mounted brigade, a battalion of colored troops (the "Cape Corps") and five artillery batteries, together with medical and other ancillary services, and a squadron of the Royal Flying Corps. The Expeditionary Force constituted about 18,700 men. Most of them thought the campaign would be over in a few months.

By March, and the arrival of Smuts, this army was prepared and waiting in its various camps.

Some people expressed surprise at the numbers of Boers in the South African force. Smuts and van Deventer themselves had been fighting many of the senior British officers they now commanded, only a few years before. Van Deventer's husky speech was the result of a British bullet in his throat. To some it seemed a strange situation. To a few it was distinctly uncomfortable. But, as a rule, there was little awkwardness or bitterness. One of the volunteers gave as his reason for going to East Africa, "I had no animus against the German people, but I thought then, as I think now, that a victorious Germany would have been a disaster . . . and I could not hang back while so many of my countrymen were moving forward to an adventure in the wilds of Africa." Another told Meinertzhagen, "Though we would sooner be under British rule than German we do not love the British. Our dream is eventual independence . . . we all hope that when this war is over we shall receive it. If you don't give it, we shall take it."

Meinertzhagen and Smuts got on well. The South African knew Meinertzhagen's family and one suspects that he was the first commander in East Africa not to be a little frightened of the energetic, ruthless intelligence chief. But Meinertzhagen thought Smuts overconfident and was dismayed to hear the Boer War hero referring to the German askaris disparagingly as "damned kaffirs."

The German forces in the north of German East consisted of 6,000 very well-trained troops, expert in bush fighting— as they had proved on a number of occasions. Eleven hundred of them were German. They were under the direct command of von Lettow-Vorbeck, who had always concentrated his personal attentions on this section of his borders. They were centered on the slopes around Kilimanjaro, in positions impossible to attack except across open ground.

Smuts knew that von Lettow, hopelessly outnumbered,

would not want an open battle, which might end the war in East Africa at one stroke. At the same time, he was himself anxious to avoid a stand-up fight and the consequent heavy casualties. He knew the effect the casualties in Europe were having on the reputations of generals there. As he said himself, he did not want the nickname "Butcher Smuts." He was by nature and instinct a guerrilla leader; a man who preferred to use his brains rather than other men's lives. He was determined to outmaneuver von Lettow from every position as quickly and painlessly as possible—without actually defeating him openly in the field. Many of the British officers thought him wrong; especially those who knew East Africa, its difficulties of communication and its disease. They thought that von Lettow should be conquered there and then, in one blow, no matter what the cost, while the South Africans were still eager and fresh. Otherwise he might not be conquered at all.

Smuts's plan was for the 1st Division under Stewart to march on Longido and then south and east round the base of Kilimanjaro. Tighe's 2nd Division and the South Africans under van Deventer were to approach west and north of the mountain, through Salaita and Taveta. This latter route lay through one of the most fascinating and beautiful parts of the continent of Africa. Plains rich with game, split by swampy rivers, gave way to swamps and thick forests. And crowning the whole area were the tremendous peaks of mountains like Meru and Mawenzi, their summits white and pink with snow and their bases sweltering in the tropics. The objective was the main German town of the area, Moshi, a large and important place by colonial standards at that time, at the head of the Usambara Railway. The intention was then to push down the railway as far as possible, through jungles and heavily vegetated country in the foothills, before the rains came.

This plan was soon in danger of collapse owing to the slowness with which Stewart's column advanced. Harassed by problems of supply, especially of water, moving forward through unfamiliar country, Stewart acted with care. Whenever they did meet slight German resistance, the troops, dusty and thirsty, were often too exhausted to give of their best. On one occasion the column would have been delayed still further if it had not been for the determined attack on a hill made by a detachment of K.A.R. under Captain G. J. Giffard, and a mounted column. Urged on by messages from Smuts, Stewart decided to leave his mounted troops, whose effectiveness in the scrub and bush was limited, and continue with infantry on foot.

The 2nd Division and the South Africans were meanwhile making good progress on the other side of Kilimanjaro. Salaita was occupied unopposed (von Lettow having decided to withdraw in face of an obviously overwhelming advance). Taveta was occupied by South African cavalry after a minor skirmish.

To clear the Germans of the area, everything depended on Stewart's appearing near Moshi simultaneously to the advance from the east. This he clearly was not going to do. Smuts told Meinertzhagen at dinner, "I am now beginning to understand how it was that we always outwitted your leaders in South Africa. Are they all like this?" On his way back to camp (twenty miles on horseback) Meinertzhagen was not only fired at by a British patrol but was chased by a lion. During the advance he was kept busy on Intelligence work; watching a suspicious Bulgarian missionary who worked in his department and whom he suspected of being a double agent (the mysterious Verbi—Meinertzhagen does not seem to have been able to confirm his suspicions); and flying in an airplane for the first time, in search of Stewart's column (which he did not see, despite their frantic waving from the ground).

After one of his personal reconnaissances, in which he frequently risked his life, Smuts realized that two small hills were going to block the advance of the force approaching from the east. He ordered a frontal attack by 1,500 men of Malleson's brigade. The action that followed was known as Latema Nek. Once the foot of the slopes were reached at midday, the attacking troops were unable to get any further without crippling casualties. It was several hours before this news reached Smuts and meanwhile Brigadier-General Malleson had decided to report sick. He said he had been suffering from dysentery all day. Meinertzhagen met him coming from the line in a car, "reclining on a soft cushion and smoking a cigarette. . . . I could scarcely believe my eyes."

By 4 p.m., Tighe had taken over command of the brigade. By this time many of the troops had been under continual fire from the hilltops for five hours. Among those killed was Lieutenant-Colonel B. R. Graham of the K.A.R.s, who had offered help to Aitken before Tanga; his body was found riddled with machine gun bullets. After reinforcements, Tighe decided on a night attack with the bayonet. This was led most gallantly by Lieutenant-Colonel the Hon. J. J. Byron, commanding a battalion of South African infantry. But near the crest of the two hills it was forced back by a fierce German counterattack. Some groups of the attackers, however, managed to reach the crest and held on until daylight. Byron himself only withdrew after being wounded and after his party of forty men had been reduced to twenty. Smuts ordered a withdrawal. While this was taking place, it was noticed that several detachments were still on the ridge. He immediately ordered every man not already withdrawing or on the hills (he found some in base) to rush to the hills in every motor vehicle available. When they got there they found the parties who had spent the night there quietly resting—the Germans having abandoned the position some time before.

The advance continued. On March 14, van Deventer's force entered the broad, tree-lined streets of Moshi, over which the snow-capped peak of Kilimanjaro towered, glittering at night like an illustration from a fairy tale. The town was deserted except for a few Greek traders and Boers. All the rolling stock had left down the line. On the same day a motorcyclist established contact with the 1st Division.

Von Lettow had taken his headquarters down the line beyond Kahe, the next settlement on the way to Tanga. He had converted a plantation hut into his G.H.Q. It "provided decidedly cramped accommodation. . . . I myself was lucky enough to find a fairly comfortable shake-down on the sofa, with the cloth off the dining-table. Telephone messages came in day and night without ceasing; but they did not prevent us from making the material side of our existence tolerably comfortable." The efforts of his boys to provide him with the fare to which he was accustomed pleased him greatly. So did the occasion when he was offered a cup of coffee prepared from the ground-down kernel of a coconut.

Von Lettow expected the next British move to be an advance down the railway line to Kahe and he accordingly had one of the *Königsberg* guns mounted there. He was delighted to hear the surprising news that another ship from Germany had broken the blockade; it had brought several thousand rounds for the *Königsberg* guns and many other supplies, but hardly any modern rifles. Under observation by three British warships for a fortnight, and its "locality" periodically shelled by them, it slipped away again unnoticed. The affair is not mentioned in the official British naval history of the war. Although the ship had only managed to reach the extreme south of the German East coastline, the supplies had all reached the army in the north—having been borne more than 500 miles by carrier. Among the stores provided by the thoughtful authorities far away in the Fatherland were clothing, tobacco, sweets and a stock of decorations, including two Iron Crosses. One went to the captain of the *Königsberg*. The other, said von Lettow, "was for me." A large quantity of trousers, which according to von Lettow "were anxiously expected," had however been captured and burned by an enterprising South African patrol (led by A. Wienholt, later a member of the Union parliament) which had penetrated behind the German lines.

There was still some time before the rains, and Smuts decided to push on down the railway. Owing to the late arrival of Stewart's force, the German battalions had been able to escape almost entirely unscathed. They had not, as the *Official History* points out, "been effectively brought to battle." And for this Stewart had to take the blame. It is, however, not at all certain that Smuts really wanted to bring von Lettow "to battle." What he had wanted was to clear all German troops from the area, and in this he had not as yet succeeded. It seemed that von Lettow was going to make him work for every position—that the German general was not just going to beat a steady retreat before an enemy which outnumbered him to an almost preposterous extent.

In order to bring up supplies for the British force, a spur of the Uganda Railway was extended south to Taveta. In a remarkable feat of engineering, in most difficult conditions, the final stretch was completed in ten days. In eight and a half "working days" ten and a half miles of line were laid, including initial survey and digging, platelaying and the construction of a three-span bridge.

Before the advance down the line to Kahe, Meinertzhagen went out on a reconnaissance. He approached to within a few yards of a camp near Kahe Station and watched and listened for some time. "I had the greatest difficulty in suppressing the feeling that every enemy soldier was expecting me and every sentry watching me." While crossing the line, in good moonlight, he was nearly caught by a sentry's wandering flashlight. Several patrols passed him almost within touching distance. "Sometimes I felt inclined to scream just to tell the enemy I was there, sometimes I was giggling at my ludicrous position, sometimes I was petrified with terror." On the way back to his own lines he had to swim a crocodile-infested river and, when almost out of German-held territory, he had to bayonet a sentry—"a beastly job but vital." He arrived back at Moshi at 10 a.m. and reported to Smuts, who only told him, "Meinertzhagen, you're mad."

The advance to Kahe began on March 18, mostly with Stewart's division and the South Africans. On the following day Stewart, finding Smuts's dissatisfaction with him obvious and impossible, resigned. In fact, Smuts had already made up his mind to relieve him of his command. Stewart returned to India. His division was given to Brigadier-

General S. H. Sheppard, formerly commanding a brigade in the same division. Shortly after Sheppard took up his command the Germans tried to stem his advance by repeated charges, with much bugle blowing and cheering. Five times they attempted to break the British line, consisting of Baluchis, Rhodesians and South Africans. Each time the charges were repulsed.

The advance, always given away by its accompanying cloud of dust, was now coming under fire from the *Königsberg* gun. The German force moved out of Kahe to take up advantageous defensive positions with each flank on the bank of two rapidly-flowing rivers. Immediately in front of their trenches was a belt of cleared bush about 1,200 yards wide covered by machine guns. The attacking troops (the columns of Sheppard and van Deventer) had therefore to advance up a strip of land bounded on each side by fast and deep rivers "full of crocodiles," as the *Official History* points out, and into heavy machine gun fire. They had got themselves into this position through the lack of a single reliable map and, one suspects, through not paying enough attention to the reconnaissances of their intelligence chief.

Casualties were heavy. An attempt to cross one of the rivers and effect a flanking movement failed. Little artillery support seems to have been given (throughout the campaign artillery support of infantry was inadequate by the standards obtained in Europe), although the *Königsberg* gun was engaged in a duel by howitzers. The men were ordered to dig in where they were for the night. In the bright moonlight the task of bringing in wounded and of reorganizing units began. Trenches were dug with bayonets, knives and hands. Most of the troops in the line were covered in filth and spattered in blood. Men called out for doctors and water. Stragglers wandered around alone, looking for anything to quench their thirst.

At dawn, Sheppard prepared to attempt another flanking movement. But suddenly it was discovered that the German positions opposite were deserted. The enemy had silently withdrawn in the night. There was not a German or an askari left. Patrols, probing down the line and into the bush, could find little sign of them. The only contact was made by some Rhodesian scouts, who encountered the last of the German rear-guard scuttling away. A hot breakfast, with porridge, had been left and the Rhodesians were grateful for it. It was realized that von Lettow's force was miles away.

The town of Kahe was empty. A road bridge had been demolished. And there, lying on the grass, was the *Königsberg* gun, left unserviceable, which had caused so much discomfort during the days that had recently passed. British artillery officers were amazed at the ingenious way in which the gun had been set up. Iron girders supported a heavy plank platform on which the gun was mounted as if on the deck of a ship. An observation post was a kind of crow's nest in the tallest nearby tree, reached by a rope ladder. An observer remarked, "The labor of carrying the material from Kahe Station and the labor of erection must have been colossal, one would think almost impossible."

No sooner had Kahe been taken than the rains came down in the torrential, soaking, dispiriting fashion common to much of the tropics. The first phase of the British offensive was at an end. The Germans had been forced from one of the most prized and settled corners of their colony. British East Africa was safe from German attack. The end of the

Usambara Railway, vital to the economy and communication of the northern area of the colony, had been captured. Some of the likeable but incompetent British officers had been removed. Stewart had left for India, after a final, angry session with Smuts. Malleson had also left, Smuts having refused to see him after his recovery. And even Tighe, still drinking, had received his orders for India. (Tighe took part in the Afghan War in 1920, but retired with a knighthood shortly afterwards—"ill health"; Stewart eventually became Governor of Aden; and Malleson got an important command in India.)

More important than all this, the pattern for the future of the campaign had been set. Von Lettow would slowly retreat, fighting just enough to weary and tax the British, never too much to suffer too many casualties himself, taking every advantage of natural cover, using every ounce of guile and wiliness he possessed to keep as large a British force in East Africa as possible. Already his 6,000 troops in the northern area had caused a good deal of trouble to the invading force of about 45,000 men.

On the other hand, it seemed that Smuts was already in the position of a steel bar to a small but powerful magnet. He seemed to be irresistibly drawn along by von Lettow. Already his careful maneuvering was causing comment among his officers. It seemed that he was in danger of losing the initiative; that the campaign would develop into the British force's merely following the German around wherever it wished to go; that not he but von Lettow was picking the places for fighting.

In his dispatch Smuts countered these charges and seemed to realize that he was in danger of losing the initiative: "Merely to follow the enemy in his very mobile retreat might prove an endless game . . . in view of the size of the country it was therefore necessary to invade it from various points with columns strong enough to deal with any combination that could be brought against them." It remained to be seen whether Smuts's plan for invasion by different columns could avoid the game of hare and hounds that he was anxious to shun and that von Lettow was anxious to promote; and whether he could by these means also avoid the full-scale battles which he shunned nearly as much.

Meanwhile, it rained.

Water fell in steady torrents. Paths became muddy streams. Camps on open plains looked as if they were floating on lakes. In the forests it seemed to drizzle into men's bones. Black clouds crowded the sky. Night and day there was the unceasing cackle of lightning and the mutter of thunder.

Giraffe, wildebeest, zebra, African carriers, and soldiers far, far away from home—all took shelter.

Chapter 6

THE LONG TREK

Smuts was impatient at the delay the long rainy season—about two months—was imposing on his advance. He occupied the time in planning an early thrust towards the Central Railway, in reorganizing the army into two divisions of South African troops and one of British, East African and Rhodesian, and with improving communications by constructing roads and bridges. There was plenty to do; and when the day's work was finished everyone huddled under cover and listened to the persistent fall of the rain.

The British division was to be under Major-General A. R. Hoskins, who had come from France to add to the bewildering covey of generals already on the scene, and the two South African divisions under Major-General C. J. Brits, on the way from South Africa, and van Deventer. Further troops had been raised in the Union and these now joined the force. It was also decided that troops from the Gold Coast and Nigeria, having dealt with the Germans in the Cameroons effectively, were to go to East Africa after a period of rest. Also, a large-scale expansion of the K.A.R., suggested by several officers in the past but always hitherto scorned, was to be initiated. Several British officers from France had arrived to join the staff—intended more for the use of Smith-Dorrien than for Smuts, who did not have a great deal of time for staff work. There were some interesting men among them and they were not calculated to make duller the already polyglot and eccentric British East African army. One, McCalmont, was the millionaire owner of Isinglass, a famous race-horse. Another, Venables, had lost his hand on the Western Front. He was able to release his artificial one by pressing on a clip at the wrist. At G.H.Q. mess one evening a Swahili waiter brought in a tray of drinks. Venables, reaching for a glass, let go the clip and left his hand on the tray. The waiter stared at it for a moment, then dropped the tray and ran out screaming, never to be seen again.

Smuts's plan was to approach the Central Railway in two thrusts. Once this railway was under his control, a large chunk of the German colony would be in his hands, with all its major towns, ports and means of communication. By using two thrusts he kept open the possibility of trapping von Lettow's force and causing it to surrender. One column, the division under van Deventer, was to march south, across the Masai Plains, first to Kondoa-Irangi, an important road junction, and then straight on to the railway. The main body, under Smuts himself, was to proceed down the Usambara Railway and then leave it to go on to the Central Railway parallel to van Deventer, by way of the township of Handeni. Smuts was convinced that von Lettow expected him to send his whole force down the railway, and therefore was confident that van Deventer's daring march through unknown bush was the decisive move of the campaign. Events were to show that he underestimated von Lettow's ability to read his thoughts.

Smuts was unable to wait until the end of the rains. He wanted van Deventer to get a good start before he himself moved. Some critics now think he would have been better to have reversed the process, as von Lettow might well have been fooled if the Smuts column, with the majority of the invading force, had started their march without there being any sign of a southerly thrust across the plains. As it was, he showed his hand. Local Afrikaner settlers assured Smuts that the rains were confined to the Kilimanjaro area. Once van Deventer got away from Moshi, they said, the rains would not be heavy enough to make any difference to military operations. He believed them. This is strange, as it was already well known that some of the most loyal supporters of von Lettow, even to the extent of fanaticism, were pro-German Boers living in German East. On one occasion two Transvaal Boers who had been captured caused surprise by goose-stepping to the interrogation table, answering nothing, and then goose-stepping away again.

Smuts said in his despatch, "The door to the interior stood wide open and unguarded."

In the last week of March, 1916, van Deventer headed the 1st South African Mounted Brigade, 1,200 strong, out of camp at Arusha and rode south in pouring rain. Harnesses creaked. Hooves splashed. Guns of the horse artillery rumbled over the muddy tracks. Cursing men continually wiped rain from their eyes. They could not know it at the time, but they were starting on one of the most notable and determined adventures of the First World War.

ON TO KILIMANJARO

The first German force to be encountered was on top of a solitary hill known as Lolkisale. It was in possession of the only spring for some miles.

Van Deventer decided to approach the hill at night, and by 9 a.m. the troops were dismounted at the foot of the hill, which proved to be about six miles in circumference with steep slopes covered in loose rocks and scrub. Soon the whole column was heavily engaged, advancing up the hill individually from boulder to boulder in typical Boer manner —firing indiscriminately at every puff of smoke from above. But soon they, and their horses in the rear, began to suffer from severe thirst. Many horses were dying of thirst and it was cruel irony that rations for the men were unable to be brought up owing to the watery, swampy conditions behind. Just as a last desperate attempt to storm the heights was being prepared by the exhausted South Africans, who had eaten little and slept not at all for forty-eight hours, the Germans put up the white flag. The garrison there, apparently, had no idea of the agonies of thirst the South Africans were undergoing.

Men and beasts drank together from the spring.

Despite the lack of horses, the Mounted Brigade moved on. At night lions roared around their camp; even the blazing campfires did not keep them away. Lions, indeed, were so plentiful in this area that some of the troops scarcely troubled to look at them when they were sighted nearby. The column continued, through the villages of flat-roofed huts of the Masai, and across the plains. Some of the troopers were disconcerted to notice the natives patiently watching them as they passed through villages, not looking at all impressed but with looks uncomfortably like ridicule.

After occupying the township of Madukani (otherwise

known as Maduk, Mbugwe, Mudikani and Köthersheim), the column met and defeated a further small German force. Tracks were rapidly becoming quagmires and the rains, which had caught up the column, showed no signs of ceasing. A fortnight after it had left Kilimanjaro van Deventer's column was reduced to 800 men. Behind it an infantry brigade was toiling on through sodden bush, mud and an almost incessant torrent of rain. Their path was littered with the putrefying corpses of hundreds of horses and mules left unburied by van Deventer in his rush forward. Attempts to get motor transport through met with frustration and failure; teams of mules and oxen were needed to release lorries from the mud. Dispatch riders were useless. The wireless broke down and the sole means of communication between mounted troops, the following infantry and G.H.Q. was by mounted messenger.

On half-rations, men and horses dropping behind every day, van Deventer forced his column on. It was as if speed was all-important to his tiny column's winning the whole campaign on its own. On April 19, after nearly three weeks of riding over swampy plains, they reached Kondoa-Irangi. Lying in a narrow valley, the town was found to be overlooked to the south by a range of rocky hills. To these the German garrison, considerably reinforced by units from von Lettow on the Usambara Railway, had withdrawn. Their position looked impregnable and clearly there were many more of them than had been expected. Before van Deventer could reach the Central Railway, they would have to be defeated.

Kondoa-Irangi was a substantial township, with a native village beside the European buildings, and a military fort. The Germans had left some of the houses in flames. The column wearily entered the town and rested in the huts and houses. Supplies were still not reaching them (even gun teams were sinking to their traces in mire) and the retreating Germans had been careful to leave no foodstuffs behind. For a time the troops lived mainly on local fruit, mostly pawpaws and groundnuts. The strength of the Mounted Brigade was now below 600. While he waited for the infantry to arrive, van Deventer consolidated the position at Kondoa-Irangi and allowed his men to recuperate as best they could. The local native chiefs were called to the town, informed that the area was now under British authority, and told that they had to provide food and carriers.

The infantry, having forded swollen rivers and struggled through swamps and floods, arrived in a very bad condition eleven days later. Many of them were ill, but they brought van Deventer's total strength to 3,000.

Even in the base area around Moshi and Arusha the tracks were impassable. One column of motor transport from B.E.A. to Arusha arrived there with forty per cent of its personnel down with dysentery. One who saw the Moshi—Arusha road mentioned "The hopeless task of making this swamp passable for wheels . . . its state was indescribable, wet black cotton soil poached to a morass. It was hard work for an unladen man to go two miles an hour . . . I saw a telegraph lorry do 800 yards in four hours." At Moshi, four inches of rain was falling in a day. Low-lying areas were becoming lakes. Bridges were swept away. Rivers flooded for miles. Camps and store dumps were soaked to the point of uselessness. But despite it all the intrepid and remarkable engineers available to Smuts had completed a railway line joining the Uganda Railway to the Usambara Railway. On April 25, the first train from Voi, on the Uganda Railway, steamed into Moshi.

Some units were beginning to disintegrate because of the

appalling conditions. The 2nd Rhodesia Regiment had to be sent back to the reasonable climate of Nairobi to recuperate, and the North Lancs., decimated by malaria and dysentery, left for South Africa for a short spell of well-earned rest.

Meanwhile, von Lettow had been reinforcing his troops near Kondoa-Irangi and, on May 9, a heavy attack was launched on van Deventer's position—askaris cheering and screaming to their own bugles, as they always did in a charge. All evening, and well into the early hours of the following morning, they tried to overrun the South African positions. But they were beaten back, despite the fact that van Deventer, knowing little of this kind of warfare, had neglected to order his troops to dig themselves in on the perimeter of the town.

This was one of the very few occasions in the campaign when the Germans, about 4,000 strong, outnumbered the British. Meinertzhagen happened to be on a visit to Kondoa-Irangi during the attack. He was amazed that van Deventer's men had got to the town at all. He wrote, "I doubt whether any British general with British troops could have planned and carried out the move in tropical Africa during the rains. Only South Africans born and bred to long distances and living on the country could have accomplished it." Meinertzhagen was impressed with van Deventer himself, "Calm and collected, divulging his plans to none, not even to his staff. He is as cunning as an old fox and does not make up his mind till the last moment—then he acts like lightning; up to that moment he appears dense and slow." Van Deventer was, indeed, a perfect man for the job on hand. Imperturbable, courageous, with as fine an eye for country and a talent for open maneuver as Smuts himself, and a dry humor. He did not have a regular staff in the

British army sense. His officers did not specialize in any particular branch; there was no red tape and few records were kept, and one gathers that at this period, at least, he had little time for Intelligence. Van Deventer was also, perhaps, the only commander throughout the campaign who refused to be overawed by the personality of von Lettow. For by now the German commander was, in an uncanny way, beginning to take on a mischievous, but at the same time oppressive, personality to men who had never set eyes on him and who had never so much as heard of him a few months previously. Officers who had seen a picture of von Lettow, or had some anecdote to tell of him, were never short of companions and listeners.

During the attack on Kondoa-Irangi, Meinertzhagen was dashing about unsuccessfully trying to persuade South African officers to stage countercharges ("lack of discipline and lack of training"). He managed to kill one of von Lettow's most able captains by cracking him on the head with his own knobkerrie ("I was furious with him for hitting me"). Some of the South Africans thought he was a thorough nuisance. It was an exciting change from routine Intelligence work at Moshi. "The night was clear but without moon, and the flashes of rifles and machine guns was a beautiful sight. The ping and moaning of bullets was not so pleasant." A bayonet charge was "a fine sight in the glare of star-shell and flares."

On his return to Moshi, Meinertzhagen reported on what had occurred to Smuts, but he was probably more interested in an intriguing piece of intelligence he had heard from one of his agents, than in official reports. He knew that the *Königsberg* had a magnificent ensign, and that when the hulk of the battleship was left in the Rufiji, this huge flag had been taken by sailors, who were now joined with an askari infantry company. Meinertzhagen had coveted this flag for many months and had laid several plots to catch it, so far with no success. But now he had heard that this company was going to raid the line of communication between Kondoa-Irangi and the Kilimanjaro area. He warned the posts on the route, but secretly concentrated 160 of his best scouts and agents, placing them under the command of a tough and ruthless Dutchman called Linton. They went off to ambush the *Königsberg* company, eventually found them and carried out a successful ambush. More than half the Germans were killed by a Vickers gun as, bunched together, they crossed a river.

Linton delivered the great flag to Meinertzhagen at his office in Moshi and promised not to mention it until the war was over. They split a bottle of champagne.

Meanwhile, something like attrition warfare had set in at Kondoa-Irangi. The Germans shelled the town from their lines on the hills, especially with several *Königsberg* guns. Van Deventer's force, of whom about 1,000 were down with fever, attempted to take some of the hills (on one occasion a South African party scaling the heights to take a German gun found, on arrival, only a piece of paper on which was written, "Fifteen rupees for the bluddy Englisch"), or, more often, spent long periods in their trenches, behind barbed wire, which stretched for some miles. At night, the South Africans could sometimes hear the words of "Deutschland über Alles" drifting over to them, as the Germans sang around their fires. If it had not been for the hot, wet weather, the occasional roaring of lions and the chirping of crickets at night, a visitor from France, that year of 1916, might almost have been reminded of somewhere else.

A small column which had marched south concurrently with van Deventer to take an unimportant village, had also reached its objective—"the one island standing out of the marsh"—after a wretched march through mud and swamp and in a continual downpour. Having got there, the little column waited for weeks for further orders. Unfortunately, they were not only completely out of touch, it seems that they were also forgotten. Soon they were on half rations and some Indians among them were utterly miserable at having to eat unaccustomed local produce. Many were ill with fever.

They waited there for three weeks.

At last a message came. It told the column to move farther south to join with van Deventer in a concerted attack planned to take place shortly. It also pointed out that the lieutenant-colonel in command was in fact junior to another lieutenant-colonel in the column, and command should be changed accordingly. Sick, dispirited and confused, the column moved off once more—across inland oceans of swamp, along tracks that were streams of oozing mud and rivers that had swollen to three and four times their normal breadth.

A relief column which should have caught up with them had been delayed. It had been "fully occupied" in dealing with cattle-raiding and local strife among tribes on the way.

At Kondoa-Irangi, the shelling and the patrols went on. The front widened. Trenches were lengthened in the soft African soil. During the day the heat was baking and intense. At night it was bitterly cold. More of those who were not already affected by fever were being overcome each day. The horses that had survived the trek would never be the same again. Of the 3,894 horses already issued to the Mounted Brigade, 1,639 had died and some hundreds of others had been sent back. The communications were still hopelessly unsatisfactory. According to the *Official History,* "the troops were often half-starved."

Artillery reinforcements for van Deventer—which were greatly needed—eventually arrived in the form of naval guns salvaged from H.M.S. *Pegasus,* which had been sunk by the *Königsberg* in Zanzibar harbor early in the war. These two ships were now nothing more than two useless chunks of rusting, twisted metal. But their guns carried on the feud, far from the sea, in the heart of one of the most remote areas in Africa. Day after day, they crashed away at each other, to little practical purpose. Two aircraft were also sent to Kondoa-Irangi. Flying there at the end of May, they could not find their destination and had to turn back. They ran out of petrol and made forced landings in the bush. When they eventually arrived at the front five days later, the airfield constructed for them was promptly shelled by a *Königsberg* gun and rendered useless. The planes were the first many of the troops had ever seen.

As May stretched toward June, van Deventer began making plans and preparations for the second half of his thrust to the Central Railway. Farther north, Lieutenant-General Smuts was ready to start his push down the Usambara line. Sometimes he must have paused to wonder whether he should not have delayed van Deventer's advance until this time as well. For not only had his troops suffered horribly and a tremendous strain been put on his whole organization, but what might have been an impossible situation for von Lettow had been turned into a simple matter of transferring troops from one front to another. The *Official History,* which gives every benefit to Smuts it can, says, "It may be that the combined movement would have resulted in an earlier and more decisive conclusion of the campaign."

Now, at long last, the rains began to ease off; then, one day, the sun blazed out across the whole territory like a blessing on all men, and a great wave of relief swept across the opposing armies.

It had been the heaviest rainy season known in East Africa in living memory.

Smuts began his push southwards down the Usambara Railway on May 22, 1916. His plan was to move down the railway nearly as far as Tanga and then strike off south, parallel to van Deventer and about 150 miles east of him, making for the road junction of Handeni. From the railway on, the advance would be through bush country completely unknown to the British. Opposing his force were about 3,000 German troops. The country was difficult. On one side of the railway, to the northeast, were the Usambara Mountains, which fell in almost sheer cliffs to the track. Clearly, there was no question of advancing through the mountains. At their base, and on the other side of the railway, was a strip of dense bush country about twenty miles wide, difficult to get through between the mountains and the Pangani River which flowed into the Indian Ocean just south of Tanga. On the left bank of the river there was, however, a strip of open ground a few hundred yards wide before the thick bush started again. Smuts decided that he would advance with two columns, one going down the railway line under Brigadier-General J. A. Hannyngton, and the other, his main force, along the left bank of the Pangani under Sheppard.

Little happened.

The columns marched on toward the sea, clouds of dust rising above them. Occasionally they were fired on by a field gun from the heights, from where they must have presented a fine target. Occasionally, advance parties met fire from German askaris as they rounded a corner. But for miles the route seemed to be deserted. Air reconnaissance, going on ahead, was able to report where small parties of Germans might effect a resistance. Sometimes they dropped a casual bomb near an isolated German position, but never, so far as is known, on one. Producing tiny craters on the vast expanses of the African Continent, the bombs were a marvel to the natives but of no consequence to the war.

"The rapidity of our advance," said Smuts, "exceeded my best expectations."

The railway, of course, had been destroyed by the Germans as they retired, and behind Hannyngton's column came three hard-worked companies of engineers who restored the line as they went. Volunteer officers, not used to working with engineers, thought the progress of the railway companies was infuriatingly slow. In fact, they relaid the line at about two miles a day, a remarkable rate in the circumstances.

The columns left the railway with little incident and proceeded southward to Handeni, with persistent but ineffectual opposition from the small, retiring German force under a Major Kraut (to whom von Lettow had handed over command in the north). On the fourth of June the Old Etonians on the staff sat round a campfire with a tin of food each, and a bottle of champagne. The nights were cold; the days long. Boots and flesh were wearing thin. No one had thought the march to the Central Railway was going to be quite like this.

Handeni, an important center of communications and local administration, was a strange place to find in the remote bush of German East. Its European houses had been built, for some extraordinary reason, in the Norwegian style.

During the rains they are said to have appeared and sounded like so many waterfalls. The town suffered from a permanent plague of rats. Sheppard's column marched into it, unopposed, on the morning of June 18. It became an important base despite its unhealthy situation. A Casualty Clearing Station was set up. The army doctor made his hospital by visiting all the planters' houses in the area and collecting beds and other essentials. "Back in triumph, we have bedsteads and soft mattresses that heavy German bodies so lately had impressed. Warm from the Hun, we brought them to our wounded. Down pillows, soft eiderdown quilts for painful broken legs; mattresses for pain-racked bodies. They were so bucked to see us coming back at night laden with the treasures of German linen-chests. It would have done your heart good to see their dirty, unwashed faces grinning at me from lace-edged pillows. Silk-covered cushions from Hun drawing-rooms . . . white paint, too, we discovered in plenty. . . . But the natives had nearly always been before us, and the confusion was indescribable, drawers turned out, the contents strewed upon the floors . . . pathetic traces everywhere of the happy family life before war's devastating fingers rifled all their treasures. Photographs, private letters, a doll's house, children's broken toys . . ." (Dolbey). A herd of cows was brought up to the hospital from far back, in order to provide milk for the patients. Francis Brett Young, the poet and novelist, a doctor who had himself collapsed with fever and was being sent home, spent his time guarding the herd from lions and Masai. He recorded how the hospital was unable to get rations for either staff or patients from the hard-pressed supply depot 100 miles away.

Handeni was an unhealthy place; many Africans there had typhoid, and this, as well as malaria and dysentery, spread alarmingly among the tired and underfed troops. Weary as they were, no one wanted to linger long in the clammy, sickly township of Handeni. And General Smuts was anxious to push on.

The advance continued—through thick bush and semi-jungle. Colonel Driscoll, commanding the Frontiersmen, wrote in the London *Weekly Dispatch* of the landscape and conditions in colorful, but not inaccurate, terms. "It's very different when you get down to the plains and the bush. I don't think any words could describe that. A vast and almost impenetrable forest so thick that when an aeroplane goes up the observer sees nothing but a great green carpet below him. And wild animals, mind you, as well as wild devils to fight; the sun burning your very flesh; the flies intolerable. Imagine a camp at night under these conditions. Round and about the lions are roaring with hunger. Hyenas prowl in the hope of snapping up a sentry or leaping in and carrying off a wounded man . . . all this sounds bad enough, but believe me, it gives you but a poor account of what it cost us to win German East."

The first important action of Smuts's advance to the Central Railway now took place; there were clear signs that von Lettow intended to effect greater resistance to the British moves. It was a month since the force had moved out of the Moshi area, and all units were very weak. The 25th Royal Fusiliers (Frontiersmen) were only 200 strong. A battalion of Rhodesians could muster only 170, and the Indian battalions averaged about 350. Nearly all of these losses were through sickness, only a handful being casualties from enemy action. A Fusilier wrote afterwards, "I have never seen men more utterly tired and woebegone."

The Germans were in a defensive position on the river Lukigura, which Smuts's force had to cross. When the main British column reached this place, it had been marching for over twenty-four hours—and on very little food. Almost incredibly, they went into battle. Most knew by June, 1916, that their praises would never be sung; that no matter what deeds of valor they fought, the world would take little notice. For they were fighting an obscure and lonely war, that many must have thought hardly mattered compared with the real "show" in Flanders and France. But orders rang out down the ragged ranks of tattered soldiers in strange and assorted headgear. Fusiliers from London, adventurers from Mexico, Kashmiris and Gurkhas, all fixed bayonets. Supported by machine guns manned by Punjabis and men from Lancashire, they cheered and charged.

The askaris and their German officers fled. It was described, officially, as an utter rout. It was the most notable success yet achieved by the column, for a simultaneous flanking action had caught the Germans as they were hurriedly trying to cross the river to safety. They had not only been beaten by courage but, for once, outwitted too.

After this, there was renewed confidence in the ability of Smuts, who was often to be seen being driven about on bumpy tracks in his shiny, open Vauxhall. Perhaps, after all, the wily von Lettow could be beaten; but for the present, the force could move no more. A camp was established a few miles south of the river, and there the men tried to regain some strength for the next lap on the march to the Central Railway. It was not easy. Meat (from oxen) was fly-stricken and had to be eaten immediately—even then it was none too good. There was little else to eat but hard biscuits and some mealie flour. Once some tins of jam, one per six men, reached the camp; they were greeted with delirious joy. Smuts, his short, pointed beard and piercing eyes less perky than they had been on arrival at Mombasa, was himself down with fever in the camp. Everyone was "delighted" to see General Louis Botha and his party from South Africa on an official visit; they spent two days at the camp. Botha's motorcycle escort was commanded by Sir John Willoughby, who had taken part in the Jameson Raid, 1896.

If only the problems of supply and health could be eased, many thought, the end would really be in sight. A second mounted brigade from South Africa had disembarked at Mombasa. Van Deventer was getting ready to renew his advance. In the south, Northey was beginning his march north into German territory. In the west, Belgians from the Congo were ready to advance in conjunction with a British force from Uganda. Soon, above all, the Central Railway had surely to fall into British hands. And what would there be left for von Lettow to do after that? There could surely be no resistance then.

Van Deventer's force, away at Kondoa-Irangi, was meanwhile finding it very difficult to discover how great or small was the German force opposing it. For two months South Africans and Germans had faced each other there, but little knowledge of the German force seeped through; one of the few pieces of information was an account of a revolver duel between a planter and a German officer which had apparently caused great feeling and controversy in the German lines—useless intelligence, but interesting gossip. All the horses in van Deventer's mounted brigade were in extremely poor shape, and mounted patrols were out of the question. Van Deventer would have liked to march—but how many troops were there opposite? His men were still in no condition to launch an offensive. He decided to wait a little longer. As a Boer War commander he knew from experience that the unexpected often helps him who waits. But it was a jumpy situation; over 200 miles from a railhead and nearly every man sick. On June 19, he sent a message to Smuts: "I consider it strongly probable that the Germans have decided to make another big attack here."

Van Deventer waited; but nothing happened.

Six days later a strong force went over and up to the German lines. They found German forces retreating, and some positions had obviously been abandoned some time before. Van Deventer's units were "in no condition to follow up this unexpected withdrawal."

Smuts's force had branched off south from the Usambara Railway before reaching Tanga, and this left that port of unhappy memory still in German hands. There appears to have been no great desire to tackle its conquest a second time, but at last, early in July, three British warships shelled the town and vicinity, and on July 3 a modest force of 500 was embarked at Mombasa to attempt to take Tanga once more. It consisted mainly of the 5th Indian Light Infantry, which had mutinied at Singapore soon after the outbreak of war.

The Indians were landed in the early morning, some of them on the same beach as on the previous occasion; it still displayed relics of that day. Carefully, they approached and entered the town. It had been evacuated; only African and Indian civilians remained. Meinertzhagen had reported that this was so nearly four weeks before, but no one seems to have taken much notice. German troops, however, remained in the surrounding bush, sniping whenever they got a chance —such as when the band of H.M.S. *Vengeance* was playing martial music in the main square.

One curious thing was discovered by the British landing

party. On the ground where the previous fighting had taken place, the Germans had put up dozens of wooden crosses, apparently to mark British graves. It was decided that the bodies were to be collected and buried together in one place with an impressive monument. But it was found that the graves marked nothing and that the ground had not, in reality, been disturbed. It seemed that the Germans had made the crosses before they left, in the hope that the townspeople of Tanga would be well treated by the British, having shown themselves to be considerate to British dead. "A dirty game and quite unnecessary," said Meinertzhagen.

Now that Tanga was, at last, in British hands, some slight easing of the supply situation was able to take place, it being by far the nearest port to the main British force under Smuts, and the most convenient base. Some considered that if it had been taken during the advance down the railway (almost certainly unopposed, according to Intelligence) much suffering in the preceding months could have been avoided.

Von Lettow himself had arrived at the Kondoa area, where he had been directing operations, and had ordered the withdrawal there, after a long and weary journey from the Usambara Railway. He had also brought the bulk of his force with him, which explained the lack of opposition to Smuts in the east. He and his staff had arrived first, after the long and weary journey over swollen rivers and through thick bush—the headman of the carriers going on ahead, dancing and singing and encouraging the porters to greater efforts; the carriers chanting in slow, monotonous rhythms; the troops felling trees to cross rivers; the whole party wading across streams up to their necks. It was a journey through little-known country. Von Lettow and his staff, in rags, were forced to change into askari clothing, for want of anything better.

Fearing gradual encirclement of his main force near Kondoa-Irangi, because of the moves from Rhodesia and the Congo, von Lettow had decided, after some weeks, to transfer his main force back again to the east, in support of Major Kraut. When this was accomplished (the forces of Kraut and von Lettow actually met just north of the Central Railway), von Lettow went off on a personal reconnaissance south of the railway to inspect the lay of the country. For he knew he would soon have to retreat in that direction. A keen cyclist, he carried out most of his inspection on bicycle, bumping along over lonely, rough paths and tracks. In this fashion, and also on foot through tall elephant grass, he covered some hundreds of miles of bush and mountain passes. In a few weeks he knew the country through which he was going to withdraw his force probably better than any living European at the time.

After a strong patrol, from which von Lettow realized that Smuts's force was about to make its final push to the railway, he withdrew his force to Morogoro, under himself, and Kilosa, under Kraut. Both these were important railway townships. During the patrol a German officer had his hat shot through by an English officer, Major Buller, son of the Boer War general. The German retaliated and wounded Buller, who was captured and taken away to hospital at Dar-es-Salaam where he was nursed to health by the wife of his former opponent—an episode typical of the campaign.

After von Lettow's withdrawal, van Deventer was soon able to leave Kondoa-Irangi. Two weeks' supply of rations had accumulated, some of the previous problems of communication were solved, and the waterlogged landscape had dried out. With mounted troops going on before, beating off the few minor detachments of askaris that remained in the scattered villages, the infantry marched to the long-sought-for goal of the Central Railway. After ten days, a small party of advance motorcyclists sighted flashes not far to the south. But this was not gunfire. It was the African sun glinting on the steel rails of the great Central Railway of German East Africa. From the fort of the small rail town and station of Dodoma, its white buildings gleaming in the sun, a white flag was flying. High above, birds swooped in the sky. There was not a sound across the vast open plains with the mountains rising away on the southern horizon. The remarkable trek of van Deventer, with his small force of British and Dutch South Africans, had struck right across one of the least hospitable parts of Central Africa. "Civilization" had come to yet another corner of the continent.

Van Deventer and his staff were met at the gateway to the fort by a German officer (described as "enormously corpulent," but so was practically every other German in British memoirs and accounts of the campaign). The official handed over the keys and a medical certificate pertaining to himself.

After a few days van Deventer decided to push on down the line towards Kilosa, as von Lettow was causing some havoc by sending trainloads of troops speeding up and down the line from one of his fronts to the other. No one could be sure at which point he was weakest at any particular time.

Smuts's force, also better off now from the point of view of supplies, had pushed on as well. Nominally it was two columns under the command of Major-Generals A. R. Hoskins and C. J. Brits; but Smuts took personal control, making even minor decisions. He was hoping for a combined attack from both his forces, with von Lettow squeezed between them, resulting in encirclement and surrender. No one, Smuts included, seems to have considered a further withdrawal south by von Lettow likely. Smuts's progress was by no means easy. The country was as difficult as any so far encountered—mountainous, overgrown with thick vegetation, and punctuated by rivers and steep escarpments. There were few heavy engagements. The Germans, with von Lettow in supreme command, made their customary retreat, holding natural barriers to Smuts's advance before their own casualties became too heavy.

Smuts was inclined to plan ambitious moves, particularly his favorite flanking operation, but in order to succeed, these plans required rapid speed of movement. They were excellent on paper, but in the mountains of German East they were next to impossible. Von Lettow found no difficulty in avoiding the push westward towards van Deventer that Smuts tried to force on him, and also attempts to cut off the German retreat. Flanking movements would not work, as Smuts and his generals were discovering, unless the enemy was at the same time heavily engaged on his front. While the force under Smuts was still struggling toward the railway, fighting more battles against nature than it ever did against Germans, van Deventer was still more than sixty miles away. Von Lettow had no trouble in selecting his stores at Kilosa and Morogoro and disappearing into the bush south of the railway into the country he had already reconnoitered. But Smuts still had hopes of catching von Lettow near the railway and bringing the long chase to a decisive end. The German commander had other ideas:

"The enemy expected us to stand and fight a final decisive engagement near Morogoro . . . to me, this idea was never altogether intelligible. Being so very much the weaker party, it was surely madness to await at this place the junction of the hostile columns."

Van Deventer, who was proceeding down the railway from Dodoma, met similarly irritating but momentary resistance at various places (with names reminiscent of stories by Rider Haggard) favorable to German defence along the line, which ran through a gorge in a chain of rocky hills. His advance was hindered by a *Königsberg* gun mounted on a train, which was able to find excellent range. Von Lettow was able to reinforce and withdraw troops in a matter of hours, making the fullest use of the railway between Morogoro and Kilosa. One of these trains, hurrying too fast around a bend, left the track and finished up halfway down a high embankment. The train caught fire, and many of the askaris traveling on it were killed or injured. The South Africans came on the scene shortly afterward, to find the wrecked carriages still smoldering, and blood-stained bandages and uniforms lying about among the bodies. (Skeletons were still lying there nearly twelve months later.) The advance continued, through tropical country of palms, bamboo and steaming heat. On August 22, the town of Kilosa was seen below, at the foot of the hills and on the edge of a plain. It was deserted of German troops, and van Deventer settled his H.Q. there. The few casualties that his force had received *en route* from Kondoa-Irangi had been due, he said in a dispatch, "to the advance being carried out by avoiding as far as possible frontal attacks." A message dropped by plane gave him the latest news of Smuts's advance.

Smuts's force experienced possibly the worst of all its

marches on the last thirty miles to the railway line. It was achieved in an equal number of hours, in extreme heat, with little water, and was hampered by serious grass fires spreading over some miles (one had been caused by a motorcycle skidding and bursting into flames). On the afternoon of August 26 the 2nd Rhodesia Regiment, with two companies of Baluchis, entered Morogoro. (Von Lettow had watched their approach, marked by clouds of dust, from the hills.) They found it had been evacuated by the rear-guard of the German force a few hours previously. For the first time when a town had been captured, a considerable number of German civilians, wounded and various noncombatants, had been left behind. Was von Lettow really going off, then, to fight a guerrilla war in the jungle? The town was in disorder and looting had taken place. Bridges had been destroyed down the line for miles. Rolling stock had been damaged, much of it beyond repair. Any stores that von Lettow had been forced to leave behind—and he had taken a great deal with him— had also been destroyed.

The great goal of Smuts's campaign had been won. The Central Railway was in British hands. But von Lettow, with an army far greater than he had possessed at the start of the war, was still at large: until he had been overwhelmed or forced to surrender, there could be no peace or settled British rule in German East Africa. He had disappeared away up the dark mountain passes that loomed over Morogoro— passes easy to block to pursuing troops. And beyond those mountains lay a hinterland of bush and swamp and wilderness stretching away to the borders of Portuguese East Africa; a wilderness of which few people, even Africans in the semi-settled area now conquered, had much knowledge.

Smuts was bitterly disappointed at the escape of von Lettow. He was still determined to catch him and refused to consider reports of the state of his troops, especially those in the body that had come down with him from Handeni. In his dispatch he wrote, "I found many proofs of the precipitate flight and demoralized condition of the enemy forces, and I decided to continue the pursuit in spite of the fact that my forces and animals were worn out with the exertions of the last three weeks and that my transport had reached its extreme radius of action." Smuts decided not even to pause at Morogoro, but to push on south of the railway as fast as he could in a last desperate hope of effecting a decision to the campaign. No one was certain exactly where von Lettow had gone, but the main post at the foot of the far side of the mountains was a place called Kisaki, and it was thought that von Lettow would be almost certain to make it his base. Accordingly, the force set off once more, into the passes of the Uluguru Mountains, which, at midday, appeared to be actually steaming in the baking heat.

So the campaign entered upon another phase. Von Lettow, outnumbered, outclassed in respect of supply and sometimes outmaneuvered, incapable of either effective offence or prolonged defense, had nevertheless successfully avoided being brought to battle. The *Official History* says, "He had rightly appreciated the military value to his country of keeping diverted from the European theatre of war the considerable manpower and extensive resources brought against him, and by a leadership and personality matching those of his British adversary, he had kept his limited forces not only in being but in good heart." Smuts, on the other hand, realized that from a British point of view a speedy conclusion to the campaign was essential—in order to free the South African forces for France. His achievement in gaining the most important part of German East Africa with so little bloodshed was a notable one, and his attempt to conquer the enemy army without enormous casualties of war a noble effort. But unfortunately his strategy had not succeeded. Its conception had been proved unsuitable to the conditions of tropical Africa. "With a keen eye for strategic possibilities, at times seemingly to the point of disregard for such fetters as the problems of movement and supply, and retaining in his own hands much that might well have developed upon a trained General Staff and subordinate leaders, he had driven forward to the very limit of his army's ability" (*Official History*). His rear-organization, sometimes overcome with problems of supply for diverse units from several races, had surmounted difficulties of almost unmanageable proportions. His engineers had worked on bridges and railways with truly astonishing speed in the most appalling conditions. His Intelligence service had supplied him with a constant stream of information. And, above all, his infantry and mounted troops had shown great endurance, courage and perseverance in a task which at times must have seemed hopeless. But by now it was clear that there was a limit to how much the South African and European units, to say nothing of the Indians, could take.

Chapter 7

A HALT IS CALLED

Continuing south from Morogoro almost immediately, Smuts's force encountered stiffer opposition than for some time previously. For von Lettow had indeed evacuated his main force to Kisaki, and a great mass of supplies had been assembled there, all of which he was anxious to transport farther south before the arrival of the British column under Smuts. The troubles of the advancing troops were increased by the onset of the "small rains," usual in September. This made the mountain tracks muddy and slippery, and almost impassable to wheeled transport. The heights, of exquisite beauty for those who had the time or inclination to see, were clad in a thick forest of tall dark-foliaged trees, with every now and then, from some high road, a glimpse of the luxuriant valleys below. About sixty miles long from east to west, they averaged fifty miles in depth and provided an excellent natural barrier for von Lettow while he organized his further retreat from Kisaki. Bloody rushes by the 57th Wilde's Rifles and the Gold Coast Regiment, which, 1,500 strong, had arrived from West Africa, stormed German-held positions across the mountain tracks. At one encounter Captain J. F. P. Butler, of the Gold Coast Regiment, who had won the V.C. and the D.S.O. in the Cameroons, was killed. For nearly the whole of the journey through the Uluguru Mountains, the troops, encountering a steady rearguard resistance from the Germans, were on half rations. The 25th Fusiliers (Frontiersmen) were forced to kill and eat a precious but much-wasted trek-ox one day when they had no rations at all. This battalion took to chewing at sugar-cane stalks in an attempt to assuage the ever-present hunger. Desperate men went out hunting—some who had never shot big game before. Giraffes, elands, elephants (for the fat)—anything would do. One "patrol" returned with ivory that it took six porters to carry.

As Smuts's advance party progressed, the remainder of the division behind them slowly followed, working on a road as it went, under Major-General Sheppard, who had been a Royal Engineer. In his customary manner, Smuts was attempting a flanking movement on Kisaki, just as at nearly all the other centers of German resistance he had met before. These movements had repeatedly failed in the past, but he continued to persist in them. Two mounted "brigades" (one was only 600 strong owing to sickness among men and horses), one under Brigadier-General B. G. L. Enslin and the other under Brigadier-General A. H. M. Nussey, were to take part. In East Africa there were any number of brigadier-generals (up to this time eighteen officers of General rank had served in the campaign), but often they found themselves commanding only a few hundred men. Behind the two mounted columns were two battalions of South African infantry, grandly entitled the 3rd Division, under Brigadier-General P. S. Beves with Major-General Brits in command. This last general had an unusual decoration on each lapel. Twisted around the gilt oakleaves of a general officer were sprigs of forget-me-nots embroidered in purple. When asked by curious officers what this signified, he replied that it had been sewn there by his wife to remind him of her while he was away at war.

This flanking force was to go round the western side of the mountains at all speed and catch von Lettow unawares. After the first few days it was found that the track that the infantry were taking was quite impassable to guns, and therefore the artillery were sent back again to catch up and join the main force proceeding across the mountains from Morogoro. It continued to rain. The bush was thick, and the grass sometimes over six feet high. The troops had no great-coats or blankets, although it was often very cold at night, and after only two days from the start they were on half rations or less. Every day more soldiers went down with malaria, which by now had affected practically everyone in the whole force to some extent, and others with dysentery and sheer fatigue.

The column under Nussey lost all contact with the outside world, the mule carrying the wireless set having fallen over a precipice on the second day out and taken the wireless with it. Nussey was consequently unable to cooperate with the rest of the force and pushed on in the direction of Kisaki as best he could. This was made more difficult by the fact that the route he had been told to take, and which was marked on his map, did not exist. Runners sent to Brits were unable to find him, although he was only a few miles away. Nussey wrote, "Over sixty per cent of my strength were dismounted and their boots and clothing were in an awful state. I had no pack mules or porters. The only roads were native tracks from one native town to another." [Collyer] Owing to lack of porters (200 that he had commandeered had escaped during a thunderstorm), he was forced to bury eighty cases of ammunition somewhere near the village of Kikeo, where they no doubt lie to this day. After several more days of slogging march, Nussey arrived in the foothills six miles from Kisaki. The white buildings of the town and the fort nearby appeared to be deserted. The only sign of life was the flutter of Red Cross flags over a hospital. Unknown to him, Brits was also preparing to launch an offensive on Kisaki from the same foothills, with the mounted brigade of Enslin. The two columns were only five miles apart. "Thus," says the *Official History*, "enclosed in the thick bush and unable to communicate, isolated therefore as completely as if separated by a week's march, each column was unaware of the position and intentions of the other."

On September 7, Brits's force moved in to take the town. Enslin and the mounted troops moved round to the flank; Beves and the infantry marched in line as for a frontal attack. Almost simultaneously with the first fire from the German positions, Beves's startled men were met by a fierce onslaught of wild bees. As at Tanga, these caused considerable dismay. There was a good deal of confusion, and the advance of the infantry was delayed. When it was at length renewed, it met with heavy fire, and still three miles from Kisaki, Beves ordered his force to dig in. The German operations here were under the personal control of von Lettow. The mounted troops had fared even worse during the day. Enslin's force, dismounted, were approaching the town from the flank as quietly as they could when they were suddenly met by a bayonet charge, and retired in confusion after heavy losses. Nussey's column, five miles away, had not heard the firing and themselves attacked the following day. Their experience was equally disastrous. Moving in to take what they thought was an evacuated town, and struggling through elephant grass, they were fired on first by a German sitting in a tree. This seemed to be a signal, for soon they were met by rapid fire and many of the troopers fell to the ground. The grass was so thick and high that it was difficult to see what was happening. After dismounting his force, Nussey continued to advance. The grass was so tall that even the sky was blotted out. The men stumbled on. An attempt was made to trample the grass down, under constant fire, in order to establish a front, as it was impossible to see more than a few feet to either side. "The heat was stifling; we had no water, and casualties began to mount," one man recalled. They were bayonet-charged by the same company of askaris that had successfully performed against Enslin the previous day; the charge was repulsed after heavy hand-to-hand fighting. The column, men and horses, had received neither food nor water throughout the day.

That evening, contact was at last made between Nussey and the force under Brits. They were forced to withdraw to the nearest water, some miles back. Next day, exchanges under a flag of truce were made between Germans and South Africans, and notifications of prisoners and wounded carried out. Parleys under the white flag, sometimes even on frivolous matters, were a common occurrence in East Africa. British prisoners were returned by von Lettow, on taking an oath that they would not fight against Germany again in the war. On this occasion, however, the South Africans were apparently suspicious of the German envoy who returned the prisoners, as they seized him, blindfolded him, and left him in the bush. The officer eventually found his way back to the German lines in an exhausted condition, after a good deal of aimless wandering about. All hope of Smuts's flanking movement at Kisaki now had to be abandoned as the men "were so worn out and depleted in numbers that there could be no question of any immediate further attack by them." (*Official History.*) Smuts, in his dispatch, pointed out that if the two columns had been able to coordinate, the capture of Kisaki would have almost certainly resulted. As it was, he now had to rely on his main force, which had almost struggled through the Uluguru Mountains and was now approaching the town through the foothills.

After a stubborn resistance from the German rear-guard lasting a day at a point approaching the town, Smuts ordered Brits to move on Kisaki once more and to threaten the German line of retreat southwards. Brits was astonished. Not only were his men all semi-invalids with fever, but they were still half starved. The ground through which he would have to go was trackless; the bush an almost impenetrable tangle of tall grass and scrub that covered the area south of the Uluguru Mountains to the Rufiji River. He appears to have ignored the command and sent his mounted force off in the only direction it could usefully go, hoping for the best. This force discovered that Kisaki had been evacuated. In fact, von Lettow had completed his evacuation many days before, and when Nussey's troops had seen the town below it was indeed deserted. But this did not mean, as the South African and British commanders had apparently supposed, perhaps a little naïvely, that the Germans had abandoned all the defensive positions in the neighborhood. As von Lettow wrote in his *Reminiscences,* "It was not advisable to occupy the fort itself . . . it was situated in the middle of a completely cleared bit of country. The enemy could, therefore, only capture it by a costly attack; but he had no need to assault it at all; by means of artillery and bombs from aircraft, he would have made it intolerable for us to remain in the cramped *boma* [fort] . . . our defences were, therefore, placed a long way outside the *boma*, covered from the view of aircraft, and so arranged that they could be occupied and evacuated unobserved."

Von Lettow had experienced considerable difficulty in getting all his stores out of Kisaki and on the track to the Rufiji area where he was planning eventually to go. These had come from Morogoro, Kilosa and Dar-es-Salaam. He tried to get the loyal natives at Kisaki to act as porters, but with little success. "The numerous inhabitants, to whom the war and the many askaris were something quite new, lost their heads and ran away into the bush." Even presents of clothing, in normal circumstances a bribe that never failed, did not move them. The Africans were thoroughly afraid of the strange new excitements bursting upon them. The several hundred pack donkeys that von Lettow had brought with him were decimated and worn out. The ox-wagons were suffering from the wear and tear. All livestock, on both sides, was suffering abominably from the uncontrolled tsetse fly. Several thousand head of cattle which had been brought to Kisaki from the north were quickly moved on to the more healthy Rufiji area. The lack of carriers for stores, which were eventually moved by all men that could be spared, explained the desperate rear-guard fighting that Smuts's force had encountered. By this time, says von Lettow, "several people were suffering badly from nerves." After the strenuous months and long marches with hardly any respite since the preceding April, his whole force was utterly worn out; men were actually falling asleep while standing up. He moved his tired force to the southern bank of the Mgeta

River, just south of Kisaki, leaving all European women behind except for a few nurses. Here, depending on supplies brought up from the Rufiiji, still about forty miles away, his main force was to stay many weeks. But no news was getting through from a force under Kraut to the west. The last contact had been through the telegraphic post at Kisaki. (Communication, apparently, had been possible by this means even for a few days after the British occupation of the town.)

The British force, now together once more, was as exhausted and sick as were the Germans. But Smuts decided to push on still farther; despite advice against such a move, he seemed irresistibly drawn along by the elusive von Lettow. The Germans, however, contrary to their usual practice, showed no signs of contemplating a withdrawal. Guns and howitzers had been brought up (almost incredibly, von Lettow still had some of his *Königsberg* guns, which had been dragged over mountains and through jungles by teams of oxen and chanting Africans). Their camp on the Mgeta was substantial and well fortified. There seemed no end to their resistance, and South Africans, British and Indians alike, who had come all the way from British East Africa, were sick of the whole campaign. Morale was low. A soldier in Smuts's force wrote in his diary, "It's difficult to keep up good spirits all round. Unfortunately there is no ration improvement, and no word of fresh kit coming. Notice shirtless men in camp with badly sun-burned backs, and men on the march without socks . . . most men are without even the solace of tobacco. . . . Sometimes, I'm afraid, I feel as if I am in prison and long for the freedom of life beyond these prison walls." Sleeping in the open, with nothing but a groundsheet, and mosquito nets a luxury, practically everyone was infected with malaria or dysentery, many with blackwater and typhoid, and thousands with jigger fleas in their feet. When they *could* get cigarettes, usually Flag or King Stork, they cost tuppence for ten at the base. Brits's force was especially weary. After trying their best to carry out Smuts's order to carry on the push, the official historian wrote of them, "His troops were by this time no longer in fighting condition. Increasingly exhausted by exertions of the preceding weeks and the continuing shortage of supplies, their numbers depleted by sickness, and almost at the end of their powers, they could do little more than hold their ground." From time to time, in the intervals from the rain which was still continuing, von Lettow's men would start a bush fire to add to the British difficulties; occasionally they mounted a small attack under cover of such fires. But apart from sniping, little now occurred on the front, for the British force was unable to carry out the wishes of Smuts. On September 26, the Commander-in-Chief ordered the force to "refrain from attacking the enemy—not only on military, but also on medical grounds." Trenches were dug; dugouts constructed. The "push" had no energy left to it.

Van Deventer's division, clothed in torn and tattered uniforms and decrepit bush-hats, and with ragged beards, had meanwhile been advancing southward parallel to the advance of the main force—but striking out from Kilosa, east of the Uluguru Mountains. They were resisted by a German force under Kraut, but the opposition was not as heavy as that experienced by Smuts's force. They were, as throughout their march from Arusha, bedeviled by problems of supply, on one occasion having to fight an action after having had no food for thirty-six hours. Horses stricken by the tsetse fly died at such a rate that enough hands could not be mustered to bury them, nor was time available to prepare them for food. "The stench of hundreds of dead animals was added to the miasma of the swamps . . . it was pitiful to see the fever-racked men dragging themselves along on foot." Here too the southward advance came to an end. "Transport and supply difficulties had become insuperable, and the troops, worn out by incessant hardship, could do no more." Huge stocks of saddles were left neatly in villages, never to be seen again.

The great thrust southwards had petered out.

While the army had been attempting to continue its advance south of the Central Railway, the coastal area had been left in the hands of the Germans. It was not until the end of August that plans were made for the capture of two ports south of Tanga: Bagamoyo, and Dar-es-Salaam itself.

Bagamoyo is about forty miles north of Dar-es-Salaam. Contrary to reports from military Intelligence, the naval authorities believed it to be strongly held. (Cooperation between naval and military was often limited and clumsy throughout the campaign.) Reconnaissance by a seaplane had revealed trenches covering the best beaches for landing. In due course, the force arrived off Bagamoyo and anchored at night offshore. There were a battleship (the *Vengeance*), a cruiser, three other warships, and various small craft. At 5:30 a.m., six small ships towed the lighters in line abreast toward the shore under heavy covering fire from the warships on to the small township, which was little more than an African village with a few European buildings. The fire was answered by a *Königsberg* gun which caused some hectic maneuvering and zigzagging before it was finally silenced. But in a half hour the landing party was ashore. It consisted mostly of naval ratings and officers, with about fifty each of Royal Marines and Zanzibar Rifles. The party "rushed" the beach and split up towards various focal points. The Governor's house was taken "without difficulty" and the *boma* was found unoccupied. The *Königsberg* gun was captured, its detachment fleeing into the bush. German reinforcements, rushing to the scene, were beaten off by naval shells. The town had been taken with only eleven casualties. Throughout, contact had been kept between shore and H.Q. afloat. Observers in the air had reported on the progress of the landing. It had been carried out, against a considerably superior force, rapidly and with the minimum of confusion.

After the town had been found clear of Germans, the inhabitants were "reassured." Most of them were found in the mission church, where the bishop had steadied the morale of his congregation by celebrating Mass.

The capture of Dar-es-Salaam remained.

A force of nearly 2,000 was assembled at Bagamoyo, with twenty machine guns, under Colonel C. V. Price. Brought from the north, it was to march down the coast supported by four warships steaming close to the shore. The march was an arduous one, in scorching heat through sandy, waterless country and the suffering from thirst was a problem. One day the 2nd West India Regiment was so overcome that it consumed the water supply intended to last the whole force three days (12,000 gallons). On the fifth day hills to the north of Dar-es-Salaam were reached, and the troops were able to look down on the town and port three miles away.

A warship flying a white flag entered the harbor with a summons to surrender. In bright early-morning sunlight the Deputy Burgomaster crossed the glistening green water in the ship's boat, boarded the vessel, and accepted the terms laid down.

The troops then marched into the capital of German East Africa and took over the town. They found it to be an attractive place of shady, tree-lined streets, with a beautiful harbor bordered by a white strip of coral and sand, with several fine stone buildings, well-spaced homes with verandas screened by mosquito gauze, soft red-tiled roofs, and its environs graced with mango trees and huge baobabs that had stood there since Vasco da Gama's soldiers had passed that way long before. Up-to-date wharves for the lighters, with electric cranes, were as impressive as anything to be seen in British Africa, and the warehouses, which had once stored produce from the plantations for Hamburg and Bremen, had been especially designed for the tropics. There were 370 noncombatant Germans there, and eighty hospital patients. The rest had all left to join von Lettow in the southeastern corner of the territory. The railway station was in ruins. The Governor's palace also stood in ruins, a reminder of the beginning of the war that seemed so long ago. The rest of the town was in good order. A number of vessels had been sunk in the harbor and considerable damage had been done to port facilities. Clearly, no immediate benefit could spring from the acquisition of Dar-es-Salaam. Much work would be necessary. But its ability to cut the supply lines, enormously stretched in the wake of the advance, was soon to be a blessing on the overwrought and testy administrative staff. (Supplies from Dar-es-Salaam started from October 4, just a month after its capture.) One of the first consignments to be shipped into the port included a large batch of Russian decorations. They were "for distribution." There was some argument about the rank of the various orders. Van Deventer, especially, was difficult to please. He only accepted the Order of St. Vladimir after Smuts had assured him it was senior to any of the others.

There was some looting in the early days of occupation, especially, according to Meinertzhagen, when the G.H.Q.

arrived, even generals being in the stampede "for pictures and every class of loot." On the arrival of G.H.Q. some of the staff were, apparently, so busily engaged collecting souvenirs from empty houses that they did not notice for some time that their servants had taken the opportunity to steal from their kit many articles of value. Brigadier-General W. F. S. Edwards, in charge of the operations on Bagamoyo and Dar-es-Salaam, lost all his silk pajamas in this manner.

Work was immediately begun not only on the port but also on the railway. It was vital to have this in working order as far as Morogoro and Kilosa, in order to relieve the great hardships that Smuts's force was undergoing. Van Deventer's supply line still stretched all the way from Mombasa via Taveta, Moshi, Kondoa-Irangi and Kilosa. In Nairobi four Ford cars had already been experimentally converted for use on the railway by having flanged wheels fitted to them. This having proved successful, more cars and lorries were similarly converted, and soon drivers of both were happily tearing along the tracks with hardly a turn of the wheel for miles. Between Kilosa and the coast the Pioneer Corps restored about sixty bridges.

All in all, the taking of Dar-es-Salaam was a great booster to morale. Especially so, perhaps, to the men of the Royal Navy. There was some controversy as to who had actually *taken* the place; the military, who had sighted it from the hills and then marched in, or the navy, who had demanded the surrender. The Admiralty Prize Court made a decision in favor of the navy, and £100,000 prize money was awarded.

There were also a cluster of small ports in the southern corner of the colony, south of the Rufiji. Smuts was intent on taking these places, as he felt strong landings there might help to corner von Lettow. For if he could not be cornered somewhere, it seemed he might be camped outside Pretoria by the war's end. Also, it was necessary to make quite certain that no means of assistance, or possibly even of escape, however remote these might be, should be left to him. Rumors of the impending departure of the by now legendary von Lettow were rampant. It was said that he had to go to the Kaiser to help him win the war. It was said that a Turkish airplane was going to be sent for him from Palestine.

After consultation with the navy, a force under Colonel Price left on the *Vengeance* and another warship to take Kilwa, the most northerly of these ports. It was occupied after hardly any resistance. Lindi, Sudi and other small harbors were similarly occupied without any difficulty. Small garrisons of Indian troops were left at each one.

Farther south still, the Portuguese (known as the "Porks" to the British troops), who had entered the war against Germany in March, 1916, had also been active. The border between their colony and German East was marked by the Rovuma River, over 200 miles south of the Rufiji. Their army of about 4,300 troops (1,500 Europeans) was mostly scattered at posts along this border, as this had frequently been the cause of controversy and some fighting in the past. Many of the Europeans, however, were hardly fit to fight German askaris, as they had only recently arrived and were only half trained and suffering from the climate. On the outbreak of war some long-disputed territory was seized from the Germans, with the help of a Portuguese cruiser and gunboat; little opposition was met. Meanwhile, a further force from Portugal, 3,000 strong, had arrived and General F. Gil was put in overall command. Smuts immediately asked him to advance northward towards the Central Railway, thus catching von Lettow, already worried by Northey's progress from Rhodesia, on all sides. This Gil was most reluctant to do, even when Smuts's cable was reinforced by one from the Portuguese Government. He complained that there were no main roads and that his transport and supply system was not adequate to the task. Besides, his Europeans, mostly young recruits, were clearly intent on going in the opposite direction; 850 of them went sick in the first few weeks after arrival. General Gil's force rapidly dwindled. Towards the end of September, he did manage to make a crossing of the river, and the Portuguese flag was planted in German soil. There he awaited further events.

Chapter 8

CLOSING IN

The moves of Smuts and the Portuguese, bottling up von Lettow in the southeast corner of the territory, had been accompanied by Northey's thrust up and westward from northern Rhodesia, and by Anglo-Belgian pressure from the west. All these were by considerably larger forces than the German Command had at its disposal, and combined during the middle months of 1916 to close in gradually on all the outlying German forces.

In the west of the colony, north and west of Lake Tanganyika, the Belgians played a prominent part. During the early months of the war their *gendarmerie* had been expanded into a small military force of 15,000, including several hundred officers and N.C.O.s sent out from Europe. Their Commander-in-Chief was General Tombeur. His plan was to move round the northern end of Lake Tanganyika, to occupy the Ruanda Urundi area of German East, and then to move south in the direction of the western end of the Central Railway and the lake port of Ujiji a few miles from Kigoma.

There were high hopes, higher in London than in Africa, that this force would cooperate with a British force being assembled in Uganda under Brigadier-General Sir Charles Crewe, which intended to occupy the important German center of Mwanza on Lake Victoria, and then also to strike southward for the western end of the Central Railway. Sir Charles Crewe, a South African politician, who had been Colonial Secretary and Secretary for Agriculture in the Cape Colony before the war, had under his command about 1,900 troops, mostly locally raised, including four companies of K.A.R.

The German troops in the whole western section of the colony, as far south as Bismarckburg, had been placed under the command of Major-General Wahle. This was a retired officer who had happened to be on a visit to his son in Dar-es-Salaam at the outbreak of war, arriving the day before the start of hostilities in Europe. He had at once placed himself at von Lettow's disposal and his experience and prestige had been of considerable value to the German Commander-in-Chief. It remained to be seen if he would show equally useful qualities in the field. He had 5,000 troops, including 576 Germans, to cover his whole massive area, with headquarters at Tabora. Clearly there was no question of withholding for long the designs of the Belgians and British, and his task was to conduct a slow withdrawal in the direction already taken by that of the main German forces under von Lettow and Kraut, i.e. to the southeastern corner of the territory.

The Belgians began a slow move into Ruanda. They were

hampered by a lack of carriers; local Africans were most reluctant to serve with them. At length, Crewe agreed to supply them with a large party of carriers, 5,000 strong, and 100 ox-wagons. This, however, did not entirely solve the difficulty as the cost of such a large force of carriers was very much more (in fact more than double) than the Belgians had thought it would be. Deadlock was reached, and after some haggling, the British Government, anxious to get the Belgian force on the move, agreed to pay the difference in costs. The Belgian advance continued, a small German force under Captain Wintgens falling back without offering much resistance. But the Belgians' supply and carrier difficulties increased as they advanced into the desolate bush, and their calls for aid from the British authorities became frequent. Eventually Smuts was forced to inform Tombeur that he would do no more for them, having enough supply difficulties of his own, until, "if ever," they reached the area south of Lake Victoria.

Before an invasion from the northwest could be launched, it was essential to ensure the capture of the port of Mwanza at the south of Victoria, as this was the only practicable supply base, communicating, by boat, with Kisumu, the railhead of the Uganda Railway. It was also the starting point of the shortest route to Tabora. (At that time, of course, there was no Mwanza–Tabora railway.) The Belgians attempted to get to this area in order to cooperate in the attack on the town to be launched from the lake by Crewe's force. Their progress, slow and with few exchanges with the enemy, was not without incident. Two companies, advancing in thick bush, suddenly came upon each other, and mistaking their comrades for Germans, opened fire at short range—with disastrous results. The defection of carriers continued. Throughout the campaign no forces, not even von Lettow's when its members were at their lowest ebb and starving, experienced such problems from mass defection. At one time 1,600 deserted. The Uganda carriers, loaned by the British, were particularly apt to quit. They, apparently, were in considerable fear of the Congo askaris, many of whom came from tribes noted for cannibalism. It was believed by the carriers that the askaris indulged in this taste among the carriers whenever supplies ran short.

After several weeks the Belgians were at last in control of Ruanda Urundi, which they had seized with hardly any opposition.

At this point everything seemed ready for a combined Anglo–Belgian move on Mwanza. But Tombeur was instructed by his government to disregard this plan and to avoid any merging of the Allied forces. He was to ensure the independence of the Belgian command and was to proceed south at once to Kigoma and the Central Railway.

Tombeur cabled back to his government suggesting that at least some of his force should help the British on the attack on Mwanza, and this he was given permission to do— so long as the rest of his force moved on to the Central Railway immediately and independently. But when it came to working on a combined plan for the seizing of Mwanza, Tombeur was unable to agree with Crewe, and decided to ignore the Mwanza project altogether. By this time, Crewe and Tombeur had developed a mutual dislike and distrust of each other. Crewe, being a politician, was one of the few military and civil authorities concerned in this obscure sector of the war who could see already that the Belgians' only aim was to claim as much of German East as they could before von Lettow's resistance collapsed.

The finale to the long history of colonialism in Africa was

being made. This was the epilogue of the "Scramble for Africa." The race to the railway had begun.

Before making an attempt on Mwanza, Crewe decided to take the small lake-port of Bukoba, which had experienced the successful and rapacious raid by British troops earlier in the war. "Carew's Flying Column," under Captain P. F. Carew, was ordered to move rapidly on the town, through sparsely-inhabited bush country. Numbering 190 of K.A.R., with some Baganda Rifles, a few scouts and two machine guns, he made a quick dash across country and found the place abandoned. (Carew used to claim, after the war, that he was the only man in the First World War to be wounded by an arrow. Von Lettow accused British irregulars and scouts of using poisoned arrows, and the Rugga-Rugga tribe, sometimes used by the Germans as irregular levies to screen askaris during an attack, used spears as well as their muzzle-loading rifles. The Rugga-Rugga were also used by both sides as runners. They would trot for hours, even days, with a split stick held in front of them, a message fixed in the split. They hardly knew the difference between British and Germans and would show messages to any white man and seek further instructions. In this way both sides occasionally captured each other's orders.)

The main British force to take Mwanza steamed down Lake Victoria on a fleet of small boats, disembarking some miles outside the town. They were greeted with shells from one of the ubiquitous *Königsberg* guns, and after a short, sharp encounter in which the German garrison was out-maneuvered, the town was entered and found to have been evacuated by the German military two hours before. The wireless mast had been sent to the ground, but there was little damage otherwise. The loss of this powerful wireless station was a blow to von Lettow. From his local stations in the southeast, via Mwanza and Damascus, he had attempted to make contact with Germany. This capture did something to improve Crewe's standing in the eyes of Smuts. His command was a political appointment, and he had been described by Meinertzhagen as "a thorn in Smuts's side" and "an incompetent gasbag." With two companies of K.A.R. and fifty scouts, Crewe decided to chase the retreating Germans in person. By nightfall he and his small party had got bogged down in thick reeds on the lake shore, and early next morning, on the Tabora "road," he was attacked by a strong German force. He withdrew to Mwanza, but was intent on wasting no time in the town, as the Belgians already had a good start in the race to the Central Railway.

Hardly even pausing for a rest day, the Belgian force, in two columns, advanced twice as fast as it had hitherto. One column went down the side of Lake Tanganyika, the other farther inland. But Wahle had evacuated Kigoma and Ujiji on the orders of von Lettow, who was able to read the Belgian intentions without difficulty. The whole German force in the west was concentrating at Tabora, in order not to be cut off piecemeal by the Allies. The Belgian flag was hoisted at Ujiji, and the Belgians now occupied a large tract of country surrounding Lake Tanganyika. It appeared that within a few months they had added greatly to their African possessions with very little cost to themselves. Ujiji and Kigoma had suffered much destruction by the Germans before evacuation, however, and not a single German or askari was taken prisoner there. The last evacuation train had, indeed, only left for Tabora two hours before the Belgians reached the railway. The Belgian force now made its way down the railway towards Tabora itself.

While the Belgians had been racing to Ujiji, Brigadier-General Crewe had been delayed by a conference with General Tombeur and the Governor of Uganda, Sir Frederick Jackson. This was held to discuss the administration of the newly-occupied territory. It took place, it seems, in a not altogether friendly atmosphere. The Belgians were anxious for a foothold in the Lake Victoria area, a long-sought-after objective of theirs. They especially had their eye on Bukoba, and General Tombeur put forward strong claims for this port. The British, however, were equally adamant and were determined to limit Belgian influence in East Africa as far as possible, while making the best possible use of the Belgian troops. They pointed out that Tombeur's force would never have got anywhere near the Lake Victoria area in the first place if it had not been for British help with carriers. In the end, Tombeur was able to sustain his claims quite well, and the final report of the conference sent to the Belgian and British Governments suggested that Ruanda, Urundi, *and* the Kigoma district should come under Belgian control, "without prejudice to any post-bellum territorial claims," and that Bukoba and Tabora should be jointly administered "under the Belgian and British flags." Few at this conference could have foreseen that within a generation Africans would themselves be asking for a say in such matters. The administrators and soldiers in Africa had made their suggestions. Now it was up to the politicians at home to argue and quarrel.

Crewe now devoted himself to reaching Tabora before the Belgians. Nearly 600 of his force and carriers were sick, not only with malaria and dysentery, but with pneumonia as well. But the Belgians were also experiencing difficulties. Not only had many bridges been destroyed but they also suffered a number of serious ambushes. On two occasions the ambushes forced them to retire, and heavy casualties were inflicted. From now on there was virtually no cooperation between the two Allied columns. Signal and communication difficulties were certainly severe, and the Belgian H.Q. later let it be known that it itself found difficulty in knowing exactly what its column marching on Tabora was doing or how far it had progressed; but the fact is that Tombeur was clearly intent on an independent seizing of this important town, the most populous in German East Africa. The British and Belgian official accounts do not always agree on every point in the remainder of the operation.

The British force made its way forward, over extremely wild and arid country, with painfully slow progress. Apart from the sicknesses already mentioned, there were now outbreaks of smallpox, the plague, and, most rampant of all, meningitis. One battalion, having lost over fifty per cent of its strength through illness and disease, was sent far back near the Uganda border, where the African tribes, enjoying the lack of customary administration and control owing to the war, were "out of control." To add to Crewe's troubles, Tombeur had renewed his requests for carriers and transport. Crewe found it expedient to give him some assistance, as this, it was hoped, would somewhat constrain the Belgians' independence.

Meanwhile, a Belgian column had been located only about fifty miles to the east of the British; the two Allied columns were neck and neck. No direct contact between the two was made. A telegraph line from this Belgian column was constructed by a British Signals section to the Belgian H.Q., and it was hoped that some sort of contact between the two columns might be kept by means of this. Unfortunately, this line was continually being broken by giraffes. Both columns moved on across the vast, barren plain towards Tabora. No opposition was encountered. It was not even known if any wandering German forces were in the area. This was a constant worry for Crewe, as his column was now isolated in the heart of one of the emptiest parts of Africa with a line of communication 120 miles long. It was only through these fears that contact between the two Allied columns was at last made, infrequent messages regarding the possible whereabouts of Germans being sent by runner.

It was two months after his force had left Mwanza before Brigadier-General Crewe was within striking distance of Tabora. But on September 25, when the column was almost in sight of the metal lines snaking across the bush, a Belgian motorcyclist arrived at the British camp and was taken to Crewe's tent. He informed the British commander that Tabora had been occupied by Belgian troops six days previously. It only remained for the unhappy Sir Charles, a bitter and disappointed man, to motor in to the town.

The Belgians had covered somewhat easier, less arid ground at a quicker pace than Crewe's force. They had even been able to live off the land when their supply arrangements broke down. They had also taken advantage of the well-stocked supplies of native villages. Their journey had been an easier one, in comparison with the depopulated and wilder country that the British had traversed farther east. They were also less hampered by red tape, staff conventions and the special needs of European and Indian troops. Moreover, they had a more dedicated approach to a race that the British commander found distasteful.

Both the Belgian columns, the one advancing down the railway and the one parallel to the British force, had arrived close to Tabora simultaneously, which indicates that General Tombeur's remarks about his lack of communications may have been a little exaggerated. All the German detachments in the west, from Mwanza to Kigoma, had retired on Tabora and were under Wahle's direct command. After three days of continuous and fairly heavy fighting near the town, the Belgian force proceeding down the railway was brought to a standstill by the German resistance. The other Belgian force had heard the firing in the distance, and hurried on. This column, too, harried by at least two *Königsberg* guns, also met strong resistance and suffered a tactical defeat by Wahle's force on the outskirts of Tabora. Wahle had boldly gambled on taking on the two Belgian columns one at a time with almost his entire force, and had succeeded in bringing both to tactical defeat and causing many casualties, making the best use of interior lines. Realizing, however, that he was heavily outnumbered, Wahle evacuated the town. Two European missionaries reported to a Belgian company commander the surrender of Tabora. It was something for which the Belgians had marched over 400 miles.

Crewe was thoroughly displeased at what he believed was wilful Belgian lack of cooperation. He wanted to know why it had taken them six days to inform him of the surrender of Tabora, as during all that time he had been preparing for its capture himself. He was told that a motorcyclist had been dispatched to inform him two days after the occupation of the town, but could not find him.

Tombeur was making no attempt to chase Wahle, the Belgian Government having laid down that he was to proceed no farther into German East than Tabora, and as the German force already had a week's start, it seemed hopeless for Crewe to attempt to catch them. There were now no German troops left north of the Central Railway. It only remained for Crewe to clear up administrative details in Tabora (such as the supply of funds for British subjects who had been interned there, and the return to Mwanza of the carriers who had accompanied the Belgians), and then to decide what to do with his force. He telegraphed Smuts to inform him of what had happened and requested further instructions.

Tabora was one of the very few places in the campaign where there were complaints from released prisoners-of-war about ill-treatment. Some of those now released complained that they had been forced to clean out the askari lavatories. One complained that he had been particularly badly treated; and the Belgians put him in charge of the German prisoners, who were then similarly treated. This situation seemed to make everyone happy—even the Germans, apparently, considering it to be only justice.

The disappointed Crewe received his instructions from Smuts. He was to disband his force, on return to Uganda, except for one battalion of K.A.R. (By October his force had ceased to exist.) He himself returned to South Africa— "ill health"—where he retired from public life. That Crewe ever got to the Central Railway at all was later seen as a fine achievement of endurance, and that Wahle had been allowed to escape was to be recognized before long as a serious setback to the Allied forces as a whole. Meanwhile, the Belgians were in Tabora. And would they ever go? (In the end they did; but they were to stay in Ruanda Urundi.)

There was an exchange of formal messages between British and Belgians. King George V sent a message to the King of the Belgians: "I desire to tell Your Majesty how highly I appreciate the loyal co-operation given my troops during the long and hard operations in East Africa by the gallant officers and soldiers of the Belgian Army. I beg Your Majesty to be good enough to convey to the commanders of the Belgian forces and their comrades-in-arms my sincere thanks for their kind message, which I have just received."

To the south, von Lettow was being similarly pressed. Smuts had asked Northey, 2,000 strong, to advance in the direction of Iringa, 125 miles southwest of Kilosa, in accordance with the general strategy of squeezing von Lettow into a corner. Northey, a determined commander, whose mission was only to "co-operate" with Smuts, was happy to follow on the small German force that had been retreating before him for some weeks. He believed in "sticking at a beaten enemy as long as there was anything left." Besides, it seemed that such German forces as there were in this area were intent themselves on withdrawing upon Iringa. Here again, the main problem was one of an ever-lengthening line of supply. But the local inhabitants were particularly friendly, and local supplies were much easier to obtain than on other fronts. Also, the country, while being remote enough, was not quite so difficult as that faced by Smuts, van Deventer, or Crewe. In this sector, as in all the others, Northey was well served by South African and other engineers in building roads and bridges. The German opposition was not strong at first; some of it consisted of seamen from the *Königsberg*, who had no experience of land fighting and were unfamiliar with conditions in the African interior. The white coats of their gunners, once neat and trim on the great battleship, were now faded and torn. They had, according to the British official historian, a preference for sleeping, most of the day.

The first large action was near a village called Malangali, where the Germans were well positioned along a ridge which overlooked the track to Iringa. Along it they had prepared a defensive system of cunningly placed trenches. They had a howitzer, outmatching the light British guns, and about 1,000 infantry. The slope was steep and two attacks were mounted against it by 1,200 South Africans and K.A.R. from the south and west. Progress was slow up the rocky slopes. Soon, attempts to storm the heights came under heavy fire. Because of the clever German trench emplacements one of the attacking detachments was soon advancing in three sides of a square. They were in full view of the defenders and were subjected to enfilade and oblique fire. The Germans put their customary move of rushing reinforcements from one section to the other into operation. In this they were helped by some knowledge of immediate British intentions through the efforts of one of them who tapped the British telegraph line. After a day's fighting the British had not gained the ridge. The night was bitterly cold. It was also uncannily quiet. The British force waited for the dawn. When it came, they were astonished to find the Germans gone.

There seems no obvious reason why the Germans should have abandoned this excellent position, which they had every possibility of holding for some time, unless it was a symptom of the general desire for concentration that, not surprisingly, seemed to afflict all the scattered German columns in 1916. Another theory is that they were apprehensive of the fierce Wehehe tribe in their rear, who were on the brink of rising against them. But this seems unlikely, for, as Northey pointed out, "as they are only armed with spears they cannot do much." It is more likely that the German force overestimated the strength of Northey.

After this hard fight and stroke of fortune, Brigadier-General Northey was diverted from his advance by Smuts in order to clear up some small German garrisons in the area, before continuing once more on Iringa. When the town was eventually reached, a company of Northern Rhodesian Police were the first to enter it, unopposed. The German force had made off to the vicinity of Mahenge to the southeast. There were fifty German women and children in the town, together with a number of Indian prisoners-of-war and some British Indian subjects who had been interned. The whole population was seriously short of food, as all food and stores that could not be taken away had been destroyed by the retreating Germans. But this unfortunate fact "was not allowed to delay the pursuit."

Northey's supply line was now 150 miles long—from his base on Lake Nyasa. This was a constant worry, as it would take only a small German force in his rear to disrupt his march completely. In this connection, also, he was worried about news of activity near Tabora and the possibility of a large force of retreating Germans suddenly descending on him. The Commander-in-Chief stated that he did not think this a serious danger and ordered Northey on to Mahenge. Here, as in the eastern sector, rains were coming again. The climate was clammy and unhealthy; the landscape, thick bush. A Rhodesian survivor recalled, "The rate of progress was about one mile in two hours, but even then the path cleared was only just sufficient for troops to move in single file. . . . If it did not rain during the day, a cold nasty rain was almost certain to fall at night. . . . In the early morning the whole country was shrouded in mist." Only occasional light opposition was met.

Northey continued to worry about the possibilities of an attack in his rear from Wahle, or a sudden encounter with Kraut's force which was known to be in the area south of Kilosa. But Smuts again reassured Northey. He felt that the Germans "did not intend or cannot retire further east." He hinted that a surrender from that quarter might be expected soon, an eventuality hardly in keeping with the German commanders who were clearly resigned, if necessary, to neverending retreat. Northey was also having considerable trouble with maps, those of his own not tallying with those of his column commanders.

A halt was eventually called in order to establish posts on the line of communication, now almost stretched to breaking point. One of his commanders wrote, "Have been on reduced rations and game for last few days; have no native rations for tomorrow." With all these problems on his mind, Northey was forced to telegraph Smuts at the beginning of October: "Further move towards Mahenge is impossible." By this time his force had increased to 3,300, practically every European of military age in Rhodesia and Nyasaland having volunteered for service in some capacity or other.

Northey's force was now stretched out, facing that part of German East still occupied by German troops, on a line from Songea to Iringa, about 200 miles long. Its line of communication was barely protected. It had no reserve, and the likelihood of further reinforcements was negligible.

It was now clear that Wahle's columns were approaching the area in their headlong retreat from Tabora.

With a pause on all his fronts, Smuts was able to put through his plan of gradually replacing the white troops by Africans under European command. After continual pressure from the medical services, Smuts reluctantly decided that this was the only course open to him. "Weakened by months of semi-starvation and fever stoically borne, exhausted by endless weeks of marching, climbing and fighting under a tropical sun, the troops, his own South Africans in particular, were falling sick in such numbers that the hospitals were overflowing, the field units reduced to mere cadres." [*Official History*] Already as one of the main lessons of the campaign, it had been realized that European troops, heavily laden and kitted, were entirely unable to give of their best in tropical conditions. All down the front they were languishing in grass-hut hospitals. The African troops had proved far more suitable. This may seem an obvious statement today, but in 1916 it was a military revelation.

[183]

The North Lancs., for instance, full strength about 900, had dwindled to less than 500 and had been sent to South Africa to recuperate. Returning after two months, 531 strong, they had soon fallen away again to 345, although suffering few casualties from enemy action. At the end of the year the battalion left for Egypt. The 25th Fusiliers (Frontiersmen), who had arrived 1,200 strong in May, 1915, were now less than 200 strong, after taking part in the long trek with Smuts's force from Moshi. The South Africans were as badly decimated. For instance, the 9th South African Infantry, which had arrived in East Africa, 1,135 strong, was now less than 120. Every other white battalion had a similar story. Meinertzhagen wrote in his diary, "What Smuts saves on the battlefield, he loses in hospital, for it is Africa and its climate we are really fighting, not the Germans." Among the first to go home was Meinertzhagen himself. Smuts had been informed by the doctors that if Captain Meinertzhagen did not have an immediate rest he "would crack up altogether." He went back to Nairobi, but, after a medical report, was sent home. Before long he was causing a stir at his new post in the War Office. His remarkable career in East Africa was at an end.

Everyone earmarked for home was glad to go.

Morale, as well as disease, was a further problem. For months on end the troops, nearly all volunteers, had marched and fought without relaxation or the hope of a day's rest, without letters from home, or even news of the war elsewhere. A survivor wrote, "We had been in the wilds for so long that we had almost forgotten there was another war, so remote did things in Europe seem from us."

Lessons had been learnt. The early optimism of Smuts and his troops had given way to a realization that they were dealing with an extremely skillful and elusive foe. The reliance on mounted troops in thick bush had given way to a distrust of all animal transport in tsetse country. And such misconceptions as the supply of heavy lorries for use in jungle and roadless bush and mountains were now less likely to occur. But Smuts still seemed to be not quite aware of the stubborn character of the man he was up against. In a somewhat desperate move he wrote at this time to von Lettow, suggesting that the latter should surrender. He wrote that "in spite of the conspicuous ability and bravery" of the German defence, the futherance of the campaign was bound to result in much unnecessary bloodshed and privation, and in the eventual German capitulation. He asked von Lettow, and Dr. Schnee, to whom the letter was also directed, to "consider very seriously whether this useless resistance should not now close in a manner honourable to themselves." Von Lettow was amazed and immediately concluded that sickness had brought Smuts's army to the verge of collapse. Both he and his staff were immensely encouraged. Governor Schnee replied to Smuts, "declining" the invitation.

But Smuts was not unduly upset. After all, von Lettow was surround on all sides by hostile forces. Once the supply situation had been improved and European troops replaced by Africans, it would only remain to close in. There was no escape for the Hun.

Chapter 9

TOWARD THE RUFIJI

The months of October, November and December, 1916, were months of reorganization. Smuts was anxious to get on the move again as soon as possible, as it was known that the heavy rains would come in March, and he wanted to reach the Rufiji and overcome von Lettow by then. It was borne in mind that the area that lay before the army was notoriously unhealthy, even more so than that already covered. It was interspersed with mosquito-infested swamps.

Although they had been last to arrive, it was the South Africans who were to re-embark first. Before the end of the year, 12,000 of them were to return to the Union. Other ranks were assembled in "camping-grounds" outside Dar-es-Salaam, with no tents or shelter and very little food. A loaf of bread—and bread had not been tasted for months—could start a battle on its own. All day queues waited to exchange their tattered and filthy uniforms for fresh ones. At ten o'clock each morning everyone paraded to hear the names called out of those to leave on the next ship. The town was out-of-bounds, except to officers, who were provided with quarters, but some troops managed to get in. One recalled, "We dispersed and went about in twos and threes gazing at the modern buildings, blinking at the wonderful brilliance of the street lights. It was queer to come upon this from the surrounding darkness of the bush. It was another world. Still weak with fever, I moved along between two companions, my arms linked through theirs to keep me from falling." The 25th Fusiliers, who were by now just a handful of men, were to be reinforced by a large draft from the U.K. Additional battalions of the K.A.R. had been formed, and the Nigerian Brigade, over 3,000 strong, was on its way. A battalion had been formed (6th K.A.R.) from captured German askaris and deserters. Some South Africans would remain with van Deventer for the time being. With this new force, mostly African, with some Indian infantry and gunners, and the Gold Coast Regiment and the Gambia Company, Smuts hoped to be able to finish the campaign in January, 1917.

The forces of Northey and van Deventer, based on Lupembe and Kilosa respectively, were static, the latter much reduced and practically ineffective through sickness and continued supply difficulties. They were far apart from the main theater, but it was hoped that Northey would be able to join up with the Portuguese near the Mozambique border and prevent any chance of an exodus of von Lettow's forces into that area. It was also now realized that these two forces would have to attempt to stop Wahle's columns from reaching von Lettow's main force north of the Rufiji. Smuts was anxious once again to outflank and surround von Lettow, despite the already well-proven difficulties of such movements in the prevailing conditions. No assistance in this being likely from Northey or van Deventer in the west, he decided to land a force at Kilwa, behind the enemy lines and march inland from there. This would be combined with a frontal assault on von Lettow's positions south of the Mgeta. Northey and van Deventer were to renew their marches southeast at the same time.

Hannyngton, who commanded a brigade on the Mgeta under Hoskins, was brought back to Morogoro to receive instructions. This itself was an undertaking of some size. At one point he and his party had to strip and swim a flooded river. The roads being unfit for any form of wheeled traffic at that time, they had to walk nearly the whole way to Morogoro. Arriving in an exhausted state, Hannyngton was told he was to take charge of the Kilwa force. This was to consist of the North Lancs. (before their departure from the campaign), two battalions of K.A.R., and two Indian battalions. They steamed peacefully down the coast and joined the small garrison left there by Colonel Price. Detachments were pushed out to a number of villages surrounding the town, especially in the hills near Kibata, which commanded the approach to the town and port. These posts were to cover the area while work proceeded on improving the harbor and building a road to another small port, Kilwa Kisiwani, fifteen miles to the south.

The small unit of German troops near Kilwa immediately reported all this to von Lettow, who realized that Smuts was about to attempt yet another turning movement and prepared to withdraw the bulk of his main force from north of the Rufiji to attack Hannyngton at Kibata—thus, he hoped, taking the sting out of this dangerous move before it was even under way. He drove the herds of cattle that he still had with him into the Rufiji, forced them to swim across, and sent them further back. Von Lettow was also at this time concerned about the fate of the columns of Wahle that he knew were trying to reach Kraut, near Mahenge, from Tabora. He was anxious that they should keep the fight going as long as possible, in order to draw attention from himself, but at the same time he knew that if his main force were to be suddenly nearly doubled it would be a very mixed blessing. For he was living in an area where there was little cultivated land, and it was not easy to feed his own force.

Wahle's forces were, in fact, now bearing down on the rear of Northey's scattered position. They were about 2,000 strong and were concentrated near Iringa, which was Northey's northernmost position. On the night of October 22/23, a German column marched through this line, cutting off Iringa from Northey. The Iringa force was consequently put under van Deventer's control. A strong party of reinforcements to this area, sent by Northey to help try to restore the situation, was ambushed and cut to pieces. The same German force then attacked one of Northey's garrisons in a small village, which after several days' gallant defence, was forced to surrender. Several supply dumps on Northey's line of communication were successfully raided, but an assault on Iringa was beaten off after many casualties on both sides.

There was great alarm throughout the area, especially as van Deventer's force was in no condition to undertake heavy bush fighting. There was plenty of confusion and on at least one occasion it seems that Germans were firing at each other. Further reinforcements for Iringa were slow in coming, as large bodies could not move along the road from Kilosa at the same time owing to the limited daily water supply in the holes on the way. Nearly all Northey's posts were attacked during this period at the end of 1916, and there was much bloody hand-to-hand fighting and bayonet work. A small

fort at Malangali was put under siege by Wahle and continuous fighting took place for several days. Northey rushed
a relief force there, partly in cars bumping across the bush
tracks, and arrived just in time on the fifth day to surprise
the Germans in the rear, causing heavy casualties.

By this time Wahle's three columns had lost touch with
each other and one of them was at last trapped and forced
to surrender. Another was ambushed crossing a ford near
Iringa and decimated. But the main force, under Wintgens
(the nucleus of his columns had come all the way from
Mwanza), with Wahle himself, managed, after many alarms
and sudden pitched battles, to reach Kraut at Mahenge.
Wahle now took over command of Kraut's force as well.
This was the first definite news von Lettow had heard of
Wahle and the western forces for four months.

There were now three main German forces. Wahle's at
Mahenge; a small one at the Mgeta under Captain Tafel;
and von Lettow's main force preparing to attack Kibata
near Kilwa. The breakthrough from Tabora had cost the
Germans nearly 750 casualties.

General Smuts now left Morogoro to inspect the forces of
van Deventer and Northey. It seems probable that if he had
done so before he would have realized the danger of the
small and scattered posts there. He now ordered a concentration of forces on Iringa (van Deventer) and Lupembe
(Northey), and the two commanders were to go to these
forward bases themselves, in readiness for the approaching
general offensive. Smuts then returned to G.H.Q. at Morogoro, took a trolley down the line to Dar-es-Salaam, and a
boat to Kilwa. On his return from Kilwa he ordered more
forces to be transferred from the Mgeta region to Kilwa, and
that Hoskins was to take over the expanded force. This meant
that Smuts had, like von Lettow, now transferred the weight

of his offensive from one front to another. The shipping of this force was itself an immense problem for the administration; shipping and facilities at Dar-es-Salaam were entirely inadequate for such a task even in peacetime, but now much of the port was out of use. At Kilwa, also, the difficulties were great. All the tracks around the town were on shifting sand; even pack-mules found the going nearly impossible. The area was unhealthy, swarming with flies, and there was an appalling rate of sickness.

Von Lettow was also having supply difficulties. He was using the Rufiji as a line of supply, but the only shallow-draught vessel on the river that could go far enough was a ship precious to the local inhabitants. The civil authorities were loathe to see it endangered by military use. "A certain amount of discussion" was necessary before they allowed him to use it for bringing troops and supplies some of the way from the Mgeta to Kilwa. The District Commissioner at Kilwa had been captured, and this also made for complications as he had his own unit of troops which were reluctant to accept orders from the local military commander. There was some friction throughout the area between the German Commander-in-Chief and the white civil population. So far they had spent the war on their plantations and had lived much as before. The blockade had worried them little as their lives were less sophisticated than those of the settlers around the two railways to the north. They had been able to continue their domestic and business lives undisturbed for more than two years. There was a good deal of discontent at this sudden invasion of columns of askaris taking the pick of their cattle and denuding their land of produce. War was something that should be fought by proper armies in Europe, they said; not in the virgin lands of Africa. The atmosphere between them and von Lettow's officers was tense.

There were also transport difficulties due to hippopotami and crocodiles, which were in their thousands in this region, and prowling lions at night, which came into the camps to attack and carry off sentries. However, soon all was ready for an attack on Hoskins's force at Kibata, and von Lettow directed the ensuing operations from the airy veranda of a local government building in the hills overlooking the scene of battle.

There was a British brigade in the Kibita vicinity, well prepared and dug-in. Von Lettow began with a barrage. His artillery included two heavy guns that had been brought up after long and back-breaking effort. Several hilltops near the British positions were soon occupied by the German force. Hoskins rushed up reinforcements from Kilwa, but more hills were taken by the Germans; and these overlooked Kilwa itself. Continual and hard fighting took place every day, and some of the hills were taken by the British. The Gold Coast Regiment especially distinguished itself, but suffered heavy losses which continued after occupation, the hilltops making excellent targets for the German gunners. Now the Germans were also dug in and behind stake entanglements. There were bayonet charges, bomb-throwing, bugle calls, and death.

Von Lettow failed to take Kibata. Keeping Hoskins's force lightly engaged, he withdrew to the swampy area southwards. Most of Tafel's force had also withdrawn, to the south bank of the Rufiji, having used up practically every crop between that river and the Mgeta. Now von Lettow was on the very brink of the wilderness. Only Wahle and Kraut in the west were in a really cultivated area, on the Mahenge plateau; and how long could they last out against van Deventer and Northey?

During the retreat from Kibata von Lettow received a

personal letter from Smuts. In it he was informed that he had been awarded the Order Pour le Mérite by the Kaiser. Smuts expressed the hope that his cordial congratulations would not be unacceptable. Von Lettow replied equally politely, although at first he was a little peeved, as he thought Smuts was referring to a medal, the Order of the Crown of the Swords (Second Class), which he already had.

Such was war in German East.

While these pleasantries were taking place, the Portuguese had been forced back across the Rovuma into their own territory by the tiny German force in that area. They left behind them rifles, machine guns, ammunition and stores. There are few records of this episode, over which a veil appears to have been drawn. It is probable that the ill-trained and inexperienced Portuguese troops had experienced as much of this remote and unhealthy place as they were prepared to.

On the Mgeta front preparations were now well under way to reach the Rufiji and force a crossing. G.H.Q. moved forward from Morogoro (Smuts always liked to be near the front during an attack); a forward depot of supplies and ammunition had been completed; and the road from the railway had been improved, although work on it was still continuous. As soon as one section of this road was completed, another slipped into a valley below. Some parts of it were supported by stakes driven into the hillside. Causeways were built across the swamps. Many thought that the Royal Engineer officers in East Africa did a better job than anyone else, and there is much to support the claim. During the staff's journey forward, the Assistant-Quartermaster-General achieved some notoriety by jumping from his car and shooting a fine leopard, and soon afterwards more big game was bagged. "What was satisfactory was that on both occasions it was possible to stop and secure the skins, which were good ones," one witness reported.

On Christmas Day it rained, and it continued to rain for forty-eight hours. All traffic on the road was suspended and operations postponed. While Smuts was making his final preparations to cross the Rufiji and join up with Hoskins's force, thus surrounding von Lettow and cutting him off from Wahle at the same stroke, von Lettow had already begun to withdraw from the net.

As well as the general advance from the Mgeta, a special column, under Brigadier-General Beves, was to make a dash for the Rufiji farther west in an isolated crossing. Smuts, who was obsessed with flanking movements, hoped in this way to outflank the German force under Tafel, as a small part in the overall flanking move against von Lettow. It was a complicated move and would have been a good one in more conventional circumstances.

A start was made in the frontal advance but had to be called off after only a few miles; the troops were by then wading in water up to their waists. The Nigerians, who were to be the main attacking force, had nearly 400 men down with pneumonia.

Orders were issued for the general offensive to begin on New Year's Day. A small enemy rear-guard was completely surprised at breakfast. In their huts were neatly made Christmas trees and the relics of Christmas and New Year festivities. Among the prisoners taken was a German doctor with five African "wives." (the German askaris took their wives with them on safari; they acted as porters as well as cooks and fraus.)

The Nigerian Brigade, under Brigadier-General F. H. G. Cunliffe, met little resistance. Enemy trenches, sighted

by airplanes, were bombarded by naval guns which had
been brought up. Later in the day resistance stiffened and
the Nigerians came under howitzer fire and a counterattack
was launched against them. A party, led by Captain Gardner, bayonet-charged the howitzer detachment, taking several prisoners and capturing the gun. Gardner was awarded
the Military Cross. The Germans were startled by the
Nigerian preference for bush matchets (*pangas*) to bayonets. Fighting continued till after dark.

The attack was continued for several days, the German
rear guard causing more trouble than their numbers would
have suggested likely. On the morning of January 4, Captain F. C. Selous, D.S.O., the famous African explorer, was
shot through the mouth and killed. He and his section had
stumbled unexpectedly on a strong detachment of German
askaris and had been outnumbered five to one. This death
of a man of exceptional kindness and gentleness was a shock
that spread not only through the 25th Fusiliers but through
the whole force. Many of the younger officers had been
aware that they were fighting beside a man who had been
an African legend when they were still boys, a man who
had been a friend of Cecil Rhodes. In khaki shorts, with no
putties, a knotted handkerchief around his neck, and a gray
slouch hat on the back of his head (he refused to wear a
sun helmet), he had not been a conventional soldier, but
he had risen from fusilier to captain in the Royal Fusiliers
in three years. Fellow officers had been surprised to come
across him in the bush, after he had taken part in an action,
hunting butterflies with a net and a specimen box. Shortly
before his death he had written home, "I shall try and hold
out to the end, if possible, or, at any rate, as long as my
health and strength last." He had been invalided back to
England in the summer of 1916, and, although aged sixty-

five, he had returned to what he knew was a nightmare war, with a draft of 400 new recruits for Driscoll's Fusiliers. By the time they had reached the front there were only 170 of them left, the remainder having fallen ill with fever *en route*.

Selous was sewn up in a blanket and buried beside comrades under a pile of stones under the shadow of a tamarind tree. The army moved on and left him there in a clearing with his friends, in wild country somewhere near the Rufiji River.

Meanwhile, Beves's column, mainly South Africans, had been forcing its way through jungle and thick bush to the Rufiji. He reached a village twelve miles from its banks, having met no opposition, on the night of the 2nd. Smuts ordered him to push on, and an advance party led by Major P. J. Pretorious, the most famous of all the scouts in East Africa, set off to make the crossing. They had already had a very tiring day, but they continued in the darkness towards the great river. Porters carried the little boats in which they were to cross the river, and signalers laid line as they went in order to keep Beves and Smuts informed. The banks of the Rufiji were reached at dawn, after a total of thirty-two miles marched almost nonstop.

Soon they were across and digging themselves in. The rest of Beves's force followed during the day. Moving south, a number of German patrols were captured unawares, and a village was taken without a fight. The Germans were amazed to find the South Africans already across the Rufiji. At the village, Beves's signalers were able to tap the German line between von Lettow's and Wahle's forces without the Germans' being aware of it for thirty-six hours.

The main force from the Mgeta had now also reached the Rufiji, but here the crossing was much more difficult. The river was broader, about 800 yards wide, and the German askaris, hidden among the foliage, were watching from the other bank. On January 5, late at night, two companies with machine guns were got across unperceived by the watchers on the far side. This was a remarkable achievement, as the convoy of boats, slipping as silently as possible through the night, was attacked by a horde of hippopotami. The crews were unable to fire at them as this would have at once given the alarm to the Germans. The beasts were kept off with some success by the troops madly prodding at them with their bayonets. One boat was bitten in two by an infuriated hippo, and others were tipped over. A number of lives were lost. The German night sentries, however, were entirely unaware of what was happening in the shadows of the moonlight.

Next day the two companies lay all day in long grass, unsuspected by the Germans. Smuts himself came to the scene and ordered another, larger crossing that night. The following morning a battalion of Punjabis were over, but by now the Germans had discovered the situation, and the Indians were heavily attacked, with nowhere to retreat to except the deadly waters of the dark, fast-flowing river. It was impossible to reinforce them by daylight, as the sniping and artillery fire of the Germans proved to be exceptionally accurate. Supporting artillery fire was given from the north bank, and the Punjabis managed to hang on, although suffering very severe casualties. More troops were sent across to the bridgehead on the succeeding nights.

Smuts also visited Beves and ordered him to withdraw his units, which had penetrated some miles south of the river, to an entrenched bridgehead close to the south bank. Why he did so is not clear; probably because of the ever-present difficulties of supply. The Nigerian Brigade, which, after the first few days, had been withdrawn from the offensive as it was found to be only partly equipped, lacking even small arms, was now fully armed, and was ordered to Beves's crossing—which looked at this time the more promising of the two. Lieutenant-Colonel West, commanding the 2nd Nigeria Regiment, protested at the formation in which he was ordered to advance in line—which was likely to result in sections' losing touch, causing confusion and panic. He was relieved of his command by Smuts and sent back to the U.K.

Northey and van Deventer were also on the move. Northey's attempt to surround the Germans facing him near Lupembe failed completely, and the Germans were able to escape without trouble to their main concentration at Mahenge. Van Deventer, who had been cursed with problems of supply since he first took up his command, was beset with them once again. Finding it impossible to advance with his full force for this reason, he was able only to use part of his total strength, and even this on half rations the whole time. There had been heavy rain here, and although the railway to Dar-es-Salaam was now in working order, it was almost impossible to bring up all the supplies needed to Iringa over flooded roads and swollen rivers. While his attack was being launched with only three battalions, the majority of his force was going in the opposite direction, toward the Central Railway, in order to get food—constantly wading through rivers breast high and more. The attacking column was soon engaged against a strong detachment of Kraut's force, which had taken up an almost impregnable position on top of a steep, glacierlike slope, on which there was no dead-ground and no easy way round. The infantry advanced under a steady and deadly fire from rifle and machine gun. The wireless broke down

(a not infrequent occurrence in German East), and orders
had to be dropped by plane. A flanking movement was soon
in difficulties. The route round the side of the hill, which
appeared to be ten miles on the map, turned out to be
twenty-five miles. Most of the supplies of the flanking movement were lost through the porters' falling off precipices on
the steep path. The frontal infantry were left on the slope-
face for two days, waiting for support from the flank. But
before the flanking movement could arrive, the German
force, as usual, packed up its equipment and left during the
night in the direction of Mahenge.

It was decided to relieve all South African troops in van
Deventer's column, and they were replaced by Indians. For
the time being this advance came to a standstill.

While Smuts's plan to cross the Rufiji, a very difficult
task, had met with brilliant success, his attempt to outmaneuver and surround his enemy by a series of interrelated
flanking movements had failed. The advance in the west had
still been unable to mount a serious offensive on the German
stronghold of Mahenge. On the Rufiji, an advance from the
southern bank was slow and meeting considerable opposition. From Kilwa, also, the advance was not nearly speedy
enough to achieve its object—even though the bulk of von
Lettow's force opposing had already retired. Even when the
thrusts from the Rufiji and Kilwa were only forty miles
apart, the Germans were still able to slip through the gap
practically unscathed.

General Beves's brigade was now to return to the Union,
in common with the other South African troops, except for
the colored Cape Corps. Most of the main force on the
Rufiji was also broken up and sent north. This area was
now left mainly to the Nigerians.

At this juncture, Smuts himself was called away from

German East. He was to represent South Africa at the Imperial Defense Conference in London. Although this assignment had been discussed for some weeks in London and the Union it came as a complete surprise in German East. His work there was unfinished, and in his personal duel with von Lettow, who by this time had an almost hypnotic effect on him, there was still no final result. His new offensive had been going for less than three weeks; there were still about six weeks before the heavy rains. There was a rumor that he had asked to leave, but this would have been out of character with Smuts and there is no evidence to support it. His departure was speedy. A few days after the announcement, he was on board ship, thin and sick with malaria, steaming out of Dar-es-Salaam harbor.

There were many who wished they could go with him.

Before leaving, Smuts publicly declared that the campaign was over, and that all that now remained to be done was to "sweep up the remnants of the enemy force." (Fendall). In London he said, "The campaign may be said to be over." This view was, not unnaturally, accepted by the War Office, but it put his successor, who was to be Major-General Hoskins, in an embarrassing position. He was expected to finish off the campaign in a few weeks. There were very few people indeed in the British force in German East who held a similar view to that expressed by Smuts.

Smuts had succeeded in taking a large tract of enemy territory, and he had done so with the minimum of casualties. On his departure, only a small corner in the southeast was still in German hands. He had, in eleven months, achieved this not only against a resolute enemy but against every conceivable difficulty of supply and with a dwindling army at times so fatigued and dispirited that only his strength of character and determination seemed to keep it going. He had worked his troops ruthlessly and hard in his attempt to gain victory.

Judgments on his campaign have been varied. Some ascertain that by avoiding a stand-up fight and sticking doggedly to his outflanking movements, he had lost more men in hospital than he would have done in open battle. They say that his anxiety to save life in battle was offset by his almost brutal attitude to the health of his troops and his distrust of experts of all sorts, including doctors. They have quoted him as exclaiming, "Hunger! Thirst! There are no such things when the success of an operation hangs in the balance." They say that if it had not been for his caution the campaign would have been won early in 1916 at Kilimanjaro; that Smith-Dorrien would have succeeded where he failed by making better use of his vastly superior numbers and forcing von Lettow to fight. They say that anyway his outflanking movements would have been better served by large-scale landings at Tanga and Dar-es-Salaam, endangering the enemy retreat and shortening the lines of communication. They claim that he was too often inclined to listen to the disconnected reports of individual Boer scouts and not enough to the professionals on his staff. They complain that in an advance he was too far forward, losing touch with the general strategy. Meinertzhagen sums up this view: "A bad tactician and strategist, an indifferent general, but in many ways a remarkable soldier."

Others claim him as a humanitarian, saying that his fear of being described as a "butcher" was a sincere and revealing one. They admit he was no professional general but say that he was a brilliant amateur with a disregard for conventions that well matched the unusual circumstances of the fight; that if it had not been for his personality, the whole force would have crumbled. They point out that it was no fault of his that his supply needs, which were almost crippling, were so much greater than those of von Lettow's lightly-equipped, more mobile askaris.

The British *Official History of the Great War*, after enumerating Smuts's achievements in the campaign, says, "Yet still the enemy, in ever-dwindling numbers, but handled with unfailing skill by a master of strategic retreat, remained in being."

Chapter 10

TO THE ROVUMA

General Hoskins prepared to carry out the general strategy already laid down by Smuts. This was for the Rufiji force with the Nigerians to link up with Hannyngton's force from Kilwa, and for a further advance to take place from the port of Lindi, 100 miles south of Kilwa, which was to cut off the retreat of von Lettow who would, it was hoped, by then be retreating pell-mell before the combined Rufiji–Kilwa forces. General Northey's column was to move in from the west towards the Lindi force. It was probably the best plan available and Hoskins had no reason to alter it. For the first time in the campaign it made proper use of the ports as bases and steppingstones in the general advance, with the consequent use of the sea as a supply line instead of nearly impenetrable bush. But in East Africa the best-laid plans were known by now to go wrong with depressing frequency.

No sooner had Hoskins taken over than the Nigerians suffered a serious setback. A strong front attack by them met, after some initial success, with an even stronger counterattack. Many of their British officers were either killed or wounded and the Nigerians fell back in a confusion which soon became a headlong rush. The carriers behind the troops stampeded away into the bush and were not seen again till the following day, all adding to the confusion. A line was held about three miles to the rear. As on previous occasions, although the Germans secured some success they were unable to follow it up to any purpose.

The rains became heavy by the beginning of February, somewhat earlier than had been expected, and before long vast tracts of the battle area around the Rufiji were impassable swamps. Roads and bridges were so damaged that it was decided to call off any further attempts at advance and many troops were recalled to the railway. There was little activity on the Kilwa front, most of the German force having now withdrawn to the Lindi area, where a large build-up of British troops was under way in preparation for the advance there. This German force had been placed under the command of General Wahle, who had been brought there from Mahenge. Wahle was proving to be of inestimable value to von Lettow. The Mahenge force had come under the command of Tafel, who had gone there from the Rufiji. Von Lettow himself was fully occupied with details of communication, supply and the hatching of further plans.

Only on General Northey's front was there much activity and here the British force continued a slow advance, carefully guarding and worrying over its enormous supply line from Lake Nyasa nearly 200 miles long—kept in operation by an army of porters.

The British journey back from the Rufiji area, which had been won with such difficulty, was an unhappy business. All question of using the river as a supply line had to be abandoned in February when it had developed into a huge torrent flowing at nearly twenty m.p.h. The advance depot was continually almost empty of supplies. Mules were dying after only a single journey. At the rainy, misty, dank front the few men left existed on such improvised delicacies as monkey's brains on ration biscuits, bush-rat pie and stewed hippo's sweetbreads. Shooting parties were organized to obtain meat, but game was scarce. The Germans in this area, too, were in great difficulties at this time. One party, after many days of aimless wandering, surrendered to the Nigerians. The askaris, starving, had dug up roots to eat. These had turned out to be poisonous, and some of them had died. The survivors were in great pain and delirious. Most of them died after surrender.

March and April continued to see little action, being months of famine on some of the fronts and of preparation on others, such as Lindi. It was not until May that the rains stopped and the land began to dry out, and that the men who had stayed in the front all those weeks, cut off from supplies, began again to know days and nights that were not one long, nagging hunger. There is no doubt that during this period many British soldiers died of starvation owing to the inability to get supplies through to them.

From May, 1916, till the Armistice and after, the campaign in German East was often known by those in it as "the hungry war."

One of the German columns in the Mahenge area, under Wintgens, was unwilling or unable to take part in the general withdrawal from that area. Its askaris were mostly from the Mwanza area and were anxious to return home, and it seems that Wintgens had some difficulty, with only a few European officers, in persuading them to march farther south to land unknown to them. It also appears that Wintgens was jealous of von Lettow, or at any rate could not get on with him.

Wintgens, unable or unwilling to join von Lettow, became a small, but to the British highly annoying, independent column. He moved fast. He traveled light. Throughout the spring and summer of 1917, he was being chased hither and thither all over German East and was the cause of considerable excitement at bases and small towns where the war had been thought to have moved on for ever months before.

Early in the year this column had several brushes with Northey's force, but after the confused fighting in this area, it suddenly turned off north—much to everyone's astonishment. It appeared to be heading straight for Tabora. There was general alarm in that township, where many of the Belgians had gone on leave or were being replaced, and considerable panic all down the Central Railway. A battalion of Nigerians and Belgian troops dashed about on the railway in the converted-lorry trains. For a time Wintgens lived unmolested in an area south of the railway, while the Belgian forces prepared to surround and attack him. It was a district rich in produce and he and his men lived off the fat of the land. Wintgens, however, fell sick and became so ill that he surrendered in order to get proper medical treatment. His second-in-command, a Captain Naumann, now took over; and Naumann proved to be an even more able vagrant than Wintgens. Eluding the Nigerians, he crossed the Central Railway and marched quickly by night in the direction of Kondoa-Irangi.

The Belgians and the British had now overcome their differences and suspicions and were prepared to cooperate with each other. The Belgians agreed not only to join in "the Naumann Pursuit," but also to take a further part in the general offensive, and to assist Northey against Mahenge and Hoskins in the southeastern area—although they made it plain that their support, in numbers, so far from the Congo, would be very limited.

Time after time Naumann seemed on the verge of capture, but each time he managed to slip through the clutches of the Nigerians and the Belgians. Brigadier-General W. F. S. Edwards was hastily put in charge of all the various columns trying to make contact with the evasive German captain and bring him to battle. Living off the land, Naumann captured a *boma* near Kondoa-Irangi, where he gained some useful supplies and ammunition. While on the third day of besieging another, he was surprised by the advance party of the Nigerians who had been chasing him. Before the main body could arrive, Naumann made off in the night. Soon he was near Mwanza, but was headed off, and he moved on. The Belgians now made contact with him, but were beaten off very severely and were so badly mauled that they were unable to give much further effective assistance in the pursuit. By now this affair was receiving some attention in the newspapers in Britain and South Africa. An astonished public at home was amazed to hear that this little force was now approaching Kilimanjaro and the town of Moshi—the pride of German East, which had been so proudly captured so long before.

At the end of May, General Hoskins was recalled and his command given to van Deventer. The reason for this was obscure at the time and is even more so now. Hoskins had certainly done nothing to warrant this action and his removal caused a good deal of bitterness among the non-South African members of his staff. It was considered a grave injustice. As one of his staff later wrote, "In January he had taken over from General Smuts an instrument—however good its material—blunted and useless for an offensive action. During his four months in command General Hoskins had restored that force." Probably there were two causes behind this action from London. One was the fact that, contrary to the prediction given by Smuts, the campaign had not been finished off in a few weeks—in fact it had not progressed at all. The effect of the rainy season on the Rufiji area had not been fully comprehended in London. Secondly, and perhaps more important, was the fact that van Deventer's appointment would undoubtedly please public opinion in South Africa; although by this time there were very few South African combatant units remaining in the campaign.

Van Deventer's first few weeks with his G.H.Q. at Dar-es-Salaam were difficult. He was still as taciturn as ever and he had difficulty in expressing himself in English to the many British staff officers. It was found necessary to carry on all business with his English-speaking staff through an interpreter.

The new appointment coincided with the end of the rains, and operations were able to begin again almost immediately. The advance was continued some way on the Rufiji, against little opposition, until a point nearly parallel with Kilwa on the coast was reached. This advance then stopped, and the line was merely held while the main advances from Kilwa, southwards, and Lindi, westwards, took place.

Von Lettow had now drawn back to the Lindi area, after a long withdrawal from Kilwa in which there were some severe engagements which caused him numerous casualties he could ill afford. He made his H.Q. at the administrative center of Liwale, about 110 miles inland from Lindi. It was a slow business. Uncertain of the resistance he might encounter from the Portuguese to the rear, von Lettow was forced to fight much of the way—but always steadily retreating and trying to hold the force from Lindi at bay while he made good his retirement. The British Kilwa force was joined by most of the Nigerians and Indians from the Rufiji, and a fierce battle was fought near Nahungu, not far from Liwale. The Lindi force was joined by the 25th Fusiliers who had returned from a rest in South Africa in time for the opening of the new offensive.

Von Lettow knew nothing of the exploits of Captain Naumann, who was now east of the Kilimanjaro area terrifying every village for miles. No one knew where the Captain was going to appear next. In September, he held up a train from Tanga on the Usambara Railway. Then he went south and approached Handeni, but chased now by mounted troops and the Cape Corps, he turned north again. Once again in the Kilimanjaro area, he was eventually forced to surrender, after half his force had been captured during an engagement with the Cape Corps. Of his original column of 800, only 164 remained, fourteen of them Europeans. They had marched, between February and October, 1917, some 2,000 miles, covering most of central German East Africa. Naumann had left behind him burned villages and acres of ruined crops.

On the Mahenge front complete Allied success had only just been missed. The Belgians had struck south from Kilosa on the Central Railway, as van Deventer himself had attempted to do the previous year, and Northey had pushed on eastward. A Belgian column was also sent to Kilwa and despatched westward to prevent Tafel's making contact with von Lettow at Liwale. The Kilosa column inflicted a considerable defeat on Tafel near Mahenge, but most of the German force managed to escape into the bush. When the Belgians entered Mahenge, a goal which had been sought for so long, it was deserted of troops and only civilians and wounded were found there. A 200-mile march faced Tafel if he was to reach von Lettow. He also had to avoid the various columns which were either trying to cut him off from the main German force or to attack him from the rear. Yet another column was despatched to finish him off—this time from Nyasaland south of Lake Nyasa through Portuguese territory. By the time this latter column eventually found Tafel, having trekked through unknown and difficult country, it was so weak that Tafel had only to brush it aside.

In a desperate attempt to join up with his commander, thus putting together all the German forces still fighting in one unit, Tafel decided to march straight to the Rovuma River—the border with Portuguese East Africa—to rendezvous there with his Commander-in-Chief.

With so many stray British columns wandering about in the southeast corner of the territory, von Lettow was in an excellent position to pick on one with his main force and to assault it before aid could reach it. For all these columns, with ever-lengthening lines of communication, reaching out for each other in the bush, were becoming isolated and laying themselves open to being surrounded.

The force from Lindi, under Brigadier-General S. de C. O'Grady, had been able to advance some of the way up the Lukuledi River in flat-bottomed craft pulled by motorboats. Under naval direction they had left Lindi on a dark night, proceeding as silently as possible upstream. "Hour after hour," one soldier said, "we crept up the wide stream with black threatening shores on either beam, and all remained quiet, and nothing stirred on land to break the stillness of the sultry night nor our pent-up expectancy . . . one heard a low, tense word or two spoken across the gloom, the muffled beat of the engines." The 25th Fusiliers disembarked in the early hours—into thick mud. This advance met with resistance from the German forces gathering there from the Rufiji area. A naval gunboat, H.M.S. *Thistle,* managed to get several miles upstream and bombarded the German positions. Soon a part of the force was surrounded—the ill-starred and disease-ridden 25th Fusiliers. Out of touch with G.H.Q. and desperate for water, they formed into a square. "Weary, powder-blackened, mud-filthy, thirsty beyond the telling," they suffered miseries before contact with O'Grady, and some relief, was made after twenty-four hours. But they were not able to push on. "For five days we lay in the confined square in our shallow trenches, drinking sparingly of foul water." [Buchanan] The porters had an especially bad time, getting few rations. At the end of the five days many of them were practically unable to walk.

Meanwhile the Kilwa force was marching down to meet up with this operation from Lindi. Among the many casualties due to malaria and dysentery was Brigadier-General Cunliffe of the Nigerian Brigade. The Germans still had artillery, which they were prepared to lug about through the very thick vegetation in this region, and on several occasions they were thankful for it. They were able to hold up the Nigerians for several days after a particularly accurate bombardment on an exposed position. "The trees above this trench were dripping blood for two days afterwards from limbs and trunks of men that had been blown up and wedged between the branches." The Germans were now aware that the white troops had mostly left the campaign, and that they were being fought by colored troops. They did not welcome this move as they knew that now they would have to fight men as well able to live in the bush as their own. The Nigerians, in a tight corner, could be a bloodcurdling sight. They shouted war cries and sometimes left their trenches to dance, shaking their rifles above their heads.

On October 15 began the last big battle of the campaign. It was a bloody and hard-fought battle of trenches, grenades, dugouts, courageous assaults on strong positions, and battalions decimated by casualties—all the classic aspects of the First World War. It was the Battle of Mahiwa— which, apart from Kondoa-Irangi, was the nearest the campaign in German East ever saw to the war in Europe. But it was fought with the temperature in the eighties, far away under the blazing African sun.

The forces from Kilwa and Lindi were only about twelve miles apart; they had almost met. The whole German force was concentrated in a few square miles, desperately trying to free itself and reach the Rovuma. Could von Lettow, who had no hope of success in taking on both British advances at once, attack one and inflict a defeat strong enough to make good his getaway before the other could arrive on the scene? That is what he attempted to do.

Neither of the attacks progressed very rapidly, and the Nigerians, far from routing the enemy, soon found themselves surrounded and in a perilous situation. In a complete square, standing almost shoulder to shoulder in four-foot trenches, they kept up a ceaseless fire on the investing Germans, who were also entrenched not far away. Rations ran out. Ammunition became very short. They waited for relief but, although they could hear firing in the distance in the pauses of their own fire, it did not come. The 1st and 4th

Nigerian Regiments and the Gambia Company lost between them 300 casualties in one day—October 16. It was the most disastrous day since the formation of the brigade. By the 17th, the men had only had half a pound of rice for four days and were starving. Everywhere bullets whined above their heads as they crouched in the trenches. "All the officers knew that if help was not forthcoming soon and the Germans gave us another day like the one just passed through, all would be up with us." The nearest water hole was in full view of the German trenches, and men maddened by thirst were continually being hit as they rushed across to get water. The trenches were dug in sand and the heat in them was unbearable. A relief column trying to get through suffered 200 casualties and had to retire. Wireless communication was kept with H.Q., but this only brought bad news. There seemed no hope of the remainder of the Kilwa force being able to break through to their aid. All depended on O'Grady's column from Lindi. Men were sleeping as they stood, despite the fumes and din. An incessant German artillery barrage was rained on the position.

O'Grady battled towards the Nigerians. By nighttime on the 17th he was within one mile of their square. On the morning of the 18th it was clear that the men were soon to die of starvation unless help came immediately. Many were falling sick. There seemed no hope of O'Grady's being able to get through to them in time, as the German askaris in the whole area were fighting with tremendous ferocity. The Nigerian column was ordered by H.Q. to make a break for it through the only gap in the German trenches. This they did under heavy fire from the German troops and covering fire from a British party that was sent up to cover their retreat. There was so much firing at this point that many men were hit by stray shots.

O'Grady's Lindi division was still heavily engaged with the force of General Wahle, and now that the Kilwa force had been dealt with, von Lettow was able to give this other force his personal attention. With five companies and two guns he marched to attack an unsuspecting British column in the rear.

All this heavy fighting was taking place in extremely unhealthy country. The air was close and oppressive. The sun beat down from a cloudless sky. One of the few men who did not appear to be overcome with heat and exhaustion was Brigadier-General O'Grady himself. He wandered about in the confused battle area, making for wherever the fighting was most heavy, and with shouts and jovial backslapping inspiring his troops. When matters were at the worst he was seen walking up and down the line, accompanied by an orderly, asking everyone if they had seen O'Mara, his dog. The African soldiers were most impressed at this coolness under fire. From time to time O'Grady would incite all those within hearing distance to "give the blighters brass, begorra!" [Downes]

Von Lettow's companies ambushed a column attempting to attack the Germans facing the Nigerians in the rear. The column was practically annihilated, the only survivors having succeeded in rushing through the askaris at the point of the bayonet.

O'Grady and the Nigerians were in contact at last, but because of the fierce resistance it was decided to withdraw. The four days fighting in the Battle of Mahiwa cost the British forces 2,700 casualties—out of a total infantry force engaged of 4,900. Their losses were, therefore, more than fifty per cent of the number of troops engaged—a terrible figure even by the standards of the First World War. The German force of 1,500 also lost heavily (519 casualties). It was one of the bloodiest battles fought in Africa with modern weapons till that time. It had lasted without intermission for four days.

The most tragic decimation of all the units involved was, perhaps, that of the 25th Fusiliers. The "Legion of Frontiersmen" had gone into battle only 120 strong, a pathetic remnant of the gay and eccentric force of nearly 1,200 that had landed at Mombasa in May, 1915. Four hundred and fifty of them had returned from the rest in South Africa. They came out of the Battle of Mahiwa fifty strong— "overwhelmed by immensely superior numbers and cut to pieces." Most of the survivors were of the original Frontiersmen who had been recruited—so it seemed to them—in a different century. Reported to be "much debilitated," they were now withdrawn from the country.

After this mauling, no further advance was attempted by the Lindi and Kilwa columns during October. Von Lettow had plenty of time in which to reorganize his force and make arrangements for further evacuation. On November 6, a column of Hannyngton's Kilwa force got on the move again and harassed the enemy rear guard. Von Lettow abandoned Mahiwa in his own time, and a general advance southward of the British forces was resumed on November 7, 1917.

Von Lettow continued to move back slowly, getting ever nearer to the Portuguese frontier. His problems were many. His men were getting through their boots at a rapid rate, owing to the continual marching. Although supplies of these and many other necessities had been brought back to this far southeastern corner of the territory, they must soon run out. Von Lettow made some experiments and discovered that while it was possible for Europeans to walk tolerable paths barefoot, once the feet were hardened, it was out of the question in pathless bush. He considered homemade sandals but found them unsuitable. He therefore ordered that boots be made and he himself took lessons in boot-making. "I succeeded, with supervision, in producing an object that at a push could be taken for a left boot, though it was intended to be a right." However, the Germans were often able to restore their kit from captured stores, and repaired boots by cutting up the many saddles they captured. The German force was now almost self-contained, living off the land as it retreated—a matter in which all were now expert—with wives and camp-followers bringing along chickens and small livestock. Von Lettow was particularly worried about the latter, as the noise from cocks crowing at dawn could give away his position. He issued an order forbidding the crowing of cocks before 9 a.m., but "it brought no relief." The largest flour mill in East Africa was in this area and it worked day and night to supply the German force.

The quinine manufactured from bark early in the war was still holding out, although preciously guarded. Bandages were now also being made from bark, the stock of linen having nearly run out. Bandages, after boiling, were used again and again, until they disintegrated. The German medical units moved with the columns, setting up temporary hospitals in makeshift grass huts, and were expected to suddenly pack up and move off again at a moment's notice. Those patients who could not be helped were left behind if there was a British column near at hand. Many German wounded found themselves at home in Dar-es-Salaam in this way.

In the midst of all his other troubles von Lettow was called upon by Dr. Schnee to send a strong force to subjugate a rebellious tribe in the few remaining square miles still under German rule. This von Lettow did, with some irritation. Schnee was still marching along with the main column, his baggage taking up all the exertions and time of a number of porters. Too proud to give up, he got on with von Lettow quite as badly as before. He seemed determined to show von Lettow that, although not himself a strong or adventurous man, he could undertake anything the German commander demanded in the way of forced marches or hardships. He fought hard to retain any authority he could.

The march continued. Askaris in torn, faded uniforms, singing their monotonous songs in their deep voices, rifles reversed on their shoulders—with the butts pointing backwards—as they always did, marched on towards the Rovuma and the expected meeting with Tafel's force. Many of them had bits and pieces of British uniforms. Most of them were hundreds of miles of grasslands, jungle and mountains from home. Behind them came the bearers, and wives with children slung from their shoulders.

On the move as well was the weird arsenal and armory of the German force, manned by sailors. It was kept some miles behind the line, but because of the constant movement it seldom had more than a few weeks of work in one place at a time, to carry out the many demands von Lettow made upon it, before it too had to pack up and trek south. Von Lettow wanted mines laid behind the withdrawal, but as there were no mines ready, this was not an easy task. Some were made from *Königsberg* shells, still being carried south, from captured British grenades and from British shells taken years before at Taveta. These were intended to go off when trodden or ridden over. There was no clockwork, and the only mechanical means available were the triggers from the many damaged rifles. It was discovered that abandoned rifles were normally defective in the butt or barrel, but that the trigger mechanism was often in perfect order. Thus the makeshift mines were made.

Although quite a large number were manufactured in this

way, they did very little damage. Most of them did not operate, some operated before they were intended to, and the remainder were mostly buried in the ground by the terrified askaris whose task it was to lay them, the safety catch usually being left on. In due course one of the chief armorers was blown up by a converted shell on which he was working, and lost an eye with multiple injuries.

The German rifles in use at this stage were still largely of 1871 pattern, antiquated compared with the ones in use by the British and Belgians. But there was a steady flow of captured British rifles and ammunition, and the plan was eventually to re-equip the entire German force with British arms. To this end the 1871 rifles had to be destroyed as they became superfluous, after shooting off all the ammunition in each unit. Old rifles were destroyed by smashing the butt against a stone and inserting the barrel between two tree trunks and bending it. Work at the "arsenal" was punctuated by occasional air raids from British biplanes fluttering about in the sky and attempting direct hits by dropping bombs over the sides of their planes by hand.

Sickness was now taking a more heavy toll of the Germans than ever before, even askaris going down as quickly as the Europeans. The area was plagued by myriads of mosquitoes and flies, and snakes were in abundance, as were poisonous scorpions. Lions and leopards were also constant hazards. The local natives were almost as unfriendly as the insects and pests. There had been a bitter rebellion there in 1905–6, which the Germans, apparently, had put down with energetic brutality. Many of the plantations had been put to flames by the Africans and these were still deserted and overgrown. Some of the villages were only half inhabited, owing to the severity of the German revenge for their own loss of life. Some of them were even as empty and desolate as they had been when left by German punishment parties eleven years before. The atmosphere was oppressive and sinister. The surviving natives looked at the marching columns of askaris with resentful, sullen eyes. Money was still being exchanged by the force, but the Africans had little interest in it. Coins had been abandoned as too heavy to carry, and before leaving the Central Railway a large quantity of paper money had been printed. A stock of it was carried in sacks in von Lettow's column. On ordinary typing paper and marked by a rubber stamp, it did not look very impressive—even to unsophisticated eyes. Such luxuries as soap were almost impossible to come by. Increasingly, the Germans themselves began to ask, " 'How long can it go on? Have we not been through enough for German East Africa?' But they carried on all the same and not one so much as thought of letting down the man whose determination alone held all together." [Kock]

There was a widespread longing to know what was happening in Europe. Many thought that perhaps this was the worst hardship of all. "Nobody has the slightest idea of what's happening in Europe. We fight in a silence, and we die with silence all round." The time of building even temporary grass huts had now passed. It was just a matter of keeping on the move—day after day, week after week, with the sound of firing far away in the distance to the rear, as the last small actions were fought on German soil. As one of the German officers jocularly said, "This war has given us a place in the sun, anyway."

There was little room left in which to maneuver before the Rovuma was reached. Wahle's column, facing the main British force, was withdrawing step by step. No word had been heard from Tafel. On November 15, the village of

Chiwata was attacked by the Nigerians, by Hannyngton's column and O'Grady's column. It was hurriedly evacuated, Wahle leaving behind about 650 Europeans and askaris who were considered unfit to carry on any longer. Stores were running very short indeed in the German force, and ammunition particularly was drastically low. Von Lettow decided that, at this turning point in the campaign, he would have to leave behind much of his force and gear before marching off with the fittest and strongest into the unknown.

All the remaining troops, apart from Tafel's column, congregated at a village called Nambindinga, a few miles from the Rovuma's bank. Here, in a large clearing, a camp, one of the biggest seen so far in the campaign, was set up. Every detachment was on its way to Nambindinga and there was fighting all the way. As two companies marched to the camp, one would withdraw more slowly, covering their retreat. By November 17, there was the rattle of machine gun fire in the woods around the camp itself. For the first time in the campaign some of the askaris who had slowly withdrawn from near the Belgian Congo, via Tabora and Iringa, could hear the rifles of those who had come all the way from Tanga and Longido. Survivors of the *Königsberg* and *Kronborg* crews, who had not seen each other for years, were scattered about in the camp. Safaris of porters, and women and children, came in during the day and all night as well. The askaris were dressed in fantastic fashion; some in English uniform, others in the remains of German uniform, others in bits of both; some had headgear, some did not—"There was no understanding why there should be so many kinds of headgear in the world," Kock remarked.

A grass hut was erected, and here the remaining medical staff examined every man, weeding out the hopelessly unfit, the men with chronic malaria, with septic wounds, with feet eaten away by jigger-fleas—weeding them out from the only half-fit. Those that were obviously near the end of their usefulness were told they were to remain behind and be taken prisoner. A few were genuinely disappointed to have to give up on the brink of new adventure; most were thoroughly relieved that at last they would be free of the merciless demands of their Commander-in-Chief.

Nambindinga was virtually surrounded by British troops. Weary British staff officers believed that von Lettow, having reached the very brink of his former territory, was preparing to lay down arms at last. Some were convinced that the campaign was over. After all, German East was now in Allied hands. Surely, they argued, von Lettow would not be mad enough to disappear into Portuguese territory?

Those askaris and officers that were to be left behind burned their rifles on bonfires; the sparks and flames lit up the whole camp scene, a mile square. Von Lettow's scouts had found a way out to the Rovuma, and the exhausted British troops who had chased him here for months were not fit to make serious efforts to stop him. On the night of November 17, he marched out into the darkness. Wrote Kock: "The campfires gleamed on fantastic shapes, black and white side by side . . . some of the shapes were barefooted, some naked torsos had cartridge belts slung across them like bandoliers, some wore topis all askew, old felt hats, or uniform caps, and some were bareheaded. Rags of every kind of uniform sprang into sight in the firelight, and were gone into the blackness again. Campfires shone back from rifle barrels, and now and again from machine guns carried between two men." Behind the askaris came the remaining stores that von Lettow was taking with him, carried by bearers moving as if in a dream. And behind them the women and children. Three hundred Europeans, 1,700 askaris and more than 3,000 bearers and followers-on marched past. The assembly and departure of the column, in the trancelike scene lit by quivering fires, took several hours. And then they were gone.

Over 1,000 askaris and Germans were waiting for the British next day, to say nothing of the many women and bearers. British troops cautiously approached the camp and then, led by officers, they were soon swarming in. The Cape Corps were among the first on the scene; in their comparatively smart uniforms and turned-up South African hats, they seemed like people from another planet. A British officer, with a dozen men at his heels, dashed about flourishing his revolver. Over and over again he shouted, "The General! Where's the General?" No one answered. At last one of the men lying sick raised his head and began to laugh. Then others began to laugh too.

Someone shouted in broken English, "The General—he's gone to hell!"

Chapter 11

IN THE WILDERNESS

While von Lettow was trekking the north bank of the Rovuma, his huge column straggling for some miles in the sun, looking for a place to cross the muddy, lazy river, Tafel, unknown to him, was not far away. This force, followed by Northey and the Belgians, had arrived at a German post only a few miles from Nambindinga, only to find von Lettow's force already fled. Coming under fire from the main British force, he headed straight for the river, followed by cavalry and the 129th Baluchis.

Tafel was almost entirely without supplies and had no knowledge as to which route south von Lettow had taken. A lone British aviator, searching for Tafel, ran out of petrol and, in order to lighten his plane, dropped all his bombs into the Rovuma. This made such a noise, followed by an equally pregnant silence, that Tafel believed British artillery had crushed von Lettow nearby. Tafel had actually started to make the crossing when his heart seems to have failed him. On November 26, much to the utter amazement of the entire British force when they heard about it, a large section of his column, over 1,000 in all, walked into the camp of the delighted Baluchis, little more than 100 strong, in order to surrender. They were followed by a messenger with a white flag, saying that Tafel and the rest of his force, over 1,500, wished to surrender as well. British observers were impressed at the orderly way in which the surrender was carried out. "The little column marched, as though on parade, to the area which had been allotted to it for its encampment, in which each company at once took up the position assigned to it. Baggage having been deposited in a most orderly fashion, the men of each company instantly set to work to construct bush-huts for their European officers, while the carriers cleared the grass and underwood with their matchets and prepared less elaborate huts for the askaris. The work was done with great rapidity and on a system which had evidently become so instinctive that each cog knew to a nicety the precise place which it occupied in the elaborate mechanism." [Clifford] Six Europeans and twenty askaris refused to join in the surrender, broke away from Tafel and actually found von Lettow a few days later.

If Tafel had made the crossing, he would, undoubtedly, have joined with von Lettow—the purpose of his long rearguard action all the way from Mahenge. At the point where he had already started to cross he was only a day's march from von Lettow, who was shortly to come on abundant supplies.

Knowing nothing of this at first, von Lettow was still trying to get across the river. There were few British troops about—only small patrols—the main British force being fully occupied in dealing with the great and sudden influx of prisoners, which greatly added to the already difficult problems of supply (even though van Deventer had realized better than Smuts that native bearers were a more practical way of bringing up supplies in roadless bush than were motor transports). On one occasion von Lettow's advance party sighted a small force of mounted troops, apparently Indian, near the Rovuma. Before he had time to do anything about them an African appeared carrying a message from them. It read, "We are English cavalry, and we want to get in touch with Portuguese infantry regiments." The surprised von Lettow ignored this friendly note and mounted a "sharp" attack on the Indians, routing them and causing several casualties.

Von Lettow soon found difficulty in keeping his long and straggling column in some semblance of order, so important if he was to maintain any degree of maneuverability. Keeping it moving steadily and in uniform file took up more and more of his time. The troops and bearers cursed him softly as he approached on his horse, waving his arms and shouting encouragement and instructions.

On November 25, 1917, the column started wading across the Rovuma. The length of the column was such that the rear guard was two days later than the advance party getting across. Von Lettow later recalled that the feeling of uncertainty as to what lay before them, and the knowledge that they were cut off from all possible outside help or support, created a feeling of recklessness and callousness in himself and his troops. Although there was a strongly held Portuguese fort on the south bank of the river less than a mile from the place where the crossing was made, many took a careful bath while making their way across—in full view of the Portuguese. Others were casually sent off on hunting parties, "undisturbed by the tactical situation."

As soon as the first reached the far bank, they came under fire. There was some brisk fighting between patrols, and when von Lettow himself reached the scene he went off to reconnoiter. He got close to the Portuguese fort and saw "men in white suits moving about, a few hundred yards away." A far bigger unit was stationed there than he had supposed; but they all seemed to be going about their business as if unaware of being in danger. Von Lettow soon discovered that on one side a thick wood ran right up to beside the fort. He decided to attack through this immediately, and the attack was made while much of his column was still crossing the river. After some shots from the only gun the German force now possessed, a light mountain gun, and a heavy fusillade from the old 1871 rifles (which threw up so much smoke that they almost acted as a smoke screen), the askaris charged in. It seems that the 900 Portuguese, under the command of a Major Pinto, put up practically no resistance at all, although they suffered very heavy casualties. Major Pinto and most of his officers were killed. Once the Portuguese were completely demoralized through the unsuspected infiltration from the wood, von Lettow's men charged in from the other sides as well. The askaris seemed to go berserk, and there was needless slaughter as they charged Portuguese and African troops, who vainly screamed for mercy. Looting was taking place before firing had ceased. There was a great quantity of food, and such delicacies as jam. Pots and barrels were furiously opened and then discarded for other even more tempting discoveries nearby. Von Lettow described the scene as "a fearful mêlée." Even the Portuguese troops already taken prisoner broke loose and joined in the plunder of their own stores. Von Lettow had some difficulty in restoring order. He shouted and ordered, but no one took much notice. He set on one of the looters and struck him seven times, but each time the man got away and immediately joined in the search for booty somewhere else. With such a large force of ill-disciplined bearers and tough askaris far from home, von Lettow and the Europeans were permanently living with the possibility of mutiny and massacre; however remote, it was always a latent fear.

When he had eventually succeeded in restoring discipline, von Lettow excitedly took stock of what the capture of the fort had brought him. It was the best haul so far made by him during the war. Especially welcome were the precious medical stores that were discovered, and several thousand kilos of European rations. He was able to re-equip half his entire force with Portuguese rifles, and a generous supply of ammunition was available for each man (during December von Lettow captured one million rounds of Portuguese small arms ammunition). There were also thirty horses and six British machine guns. After reclothing his force in Portuguese uniforms, von Lettow marched off, using the Portuguese native troops as bearers for the extra supplies and leaving 150 unhappy Portuguese, wearing the discarded German uniforms, behind in the looted fort.

Marching south, along a rough native track, the long column entered into unmapped territory in Portuguese East Africa.

After every two hours of marching, half an hour's halt was called to enable the main column to close up and for von Lettow to keep control. Six hours' marching was done each day, during which fifteen to twenty miles were covered. An advance guard went on a day's march ahead, the rear-guard a day's march behind. The main force was divided into detachments of three companies, each with its own supply train and field hospital. At the head of each detachment was a heavily-armed machine gun section. The askaris marched proudly erect, their rifles reversed, chattering continually; after the raiding of a small camp, cigarette smoke would rise from all sides. Patrols probed out to the sides, looking for native guides, supplies and game. In these parts, however, there were very few inhabitants (large areas were discovered to be devoid of all population) and supplies were scarce— but there was some game, especially antelopes and guinea fowl. One after another, the horses and mules found their way into the stewpots.

During the halts a rough table was erected from branches and logs for von Lettow and his staff, and reconnaissance reports and reports from advance and rear were brought in (the head of the column investigated every trail for some distance). The evening meal was eaten round a glowing campfire, with officers invited from other parts of the column. Visitors sat on cases, von Lettow and the more senior officers on deck chairs. Then they slept in the open or in hastily-made grass huts; the Europeans always under mosquito nets.

In the morning, after a quick meal, loads were picked up, rifles shouldered, and the whole force would move off once more. No one knew exactly where they were going, not even the Commander-in-Chief himself. No one knew what was going to happen that day. Would they meet opposition? Would they fall into an ambush and be forced to surrender? Would they come to some uncrossable canyon or river? Above all, would they find more supplies, especially food?

No one could tell.

Wives and children of the askaris followed behind each detachment. The women carried the belongings of themselves and their husbands on their heads, and many had small children slung on their backs as well. A week never passed without a baby's being born. The women were kept in order by a European assisted by a few askaris. They all enjoyed gay colors, and the whole column, stretching several miles from beginning to end, resembled a gay carnival procession more than the last German force still fighting outside Europe—a force whose purpose was war and death.

The British were making desperate efforts to catch up von Lettow—to follow him, keep contact, and to engage him. The more vigor with which this campaign was carried out, however, the more likelihood there was of the British troops' dying of starvation. Dar-es-Salaam was a long way off and there was no question of living off the land when following such scavengers as the German askaris, who by now, after three years, were thoroughly expert and experienced. Also, there were, at first, political difficulties with the Portuguese, who suggested they could deal themselves with the enemy in P.E.A.

To make matters worse, no one was quite sure whether the war in East Africa was over or not.

On November 30, George V sent a cable to General van Deventer: "I heartily congratulate you and the troops under your command on having driven the remaining forces of the enemy out of German East Africa." Six days later van Deventer, ex-Boer patriot, answered, "I beg to tender the loyal and heart-felt thanks of the East African forces for Your Majesty's most gracious message, which has given the liveliest satisfaction to all ranks and has more than compensated us for the hardships and difficulties of the East African campaign." No one, at the time, had any suspicion that van Deventer might have composed the message, in Afrikaans, with tongue in cheek.

A satisfaction quite as lively as the King's message was provided for the remainder of the bone-protruding South African troops still at Dar-es-Salaam by the sight of more troopships steaming into the bay. Some found it almost incredible to believe, after slogging through swamps, jungles and mountain passes, that they were really going home at last.

On December 5, van Deventer received another cable. This time it was from a man whom he had been recently fighting in a bitter and bloody war, General Sir Douglas Haig. It read, "On behalf of the British armies in France I send you and the gallant troops under your command our heartiest congratulations on having completed the conquest of the last German colony." Van Deventer replied in suitable terms. The British armies in France and Flanders knew nothing of this message, and they would have cared nothing if they had—they had just suffered a quarter of a million casualties in capturing an insignificant village called Passchendaele.

A small engagement took place at the Rovuma between Indian cavalry and a rear-guard left behind by von Lettow to cover Tafel's crossing of the river, should he arrive. The German officer in command, who was desperately sick, gave himself up, but most of his askaris got away. Through some inexplicable oversight von Lettow's own kit and personal papers had been left with this force by mistake, and, much to von Lettow's relief, they eventually reached him. The Indians did not follow up strongly, believing they were in touch with the main rear-guard, instead of just an isolated party. The German officer later told his captors that if von Lettow's kit had been taken the German commander might well have given up the fight; he did not enjoy doing without such comforts as he could take along.

The main German force had at least two days' clear start.

Two Nigerian battalions crossed the Rovuma and began probing the unknown hinterland of Portuguese East Africa, together with a mounted column and Intelligence scouts. Attempts were made to liaise with the few Portuguese posts in the region. Little progress of any sort was made. Von Lettow was, as everyone knew, miles away—possibly even fifty miles, through thick bush and jungle.

Besides, no one really seemed to care what the man did any more.

Van Deventer, giving up all hope of von Lettow's ever getting tired of it all, made a rather forlorn approach to Dr. Schnee, whom, it was known, did not always agree with the military commander. An officer of the Nigerians, under a flag of truce, made contact with the German rear-guard after some days' forced marching. He handed over a personal letter from van Deventer to Schnee. The British Commander-in-Chief informed the Governor that his ex-colony had now been annexed by the Allies. Would it not be sensible for the German forces to lay down their arms? There was no reply.

Just before Christmas, 1917, the Nigerian Brigade and the Kashmiri artillery took part in a race meeting for two silver cups presented by their commanding officers. It took place on the northern banks of the Rovuma, with Union Jacks flying lazily in such little wind as there was and officers relaxing over bottles recently brought up, in the cool shade of tents. There was a flat race and a steeplechase. There was also a mule race for "the natives." The latter was, said a senior spectator, "most amusing to watch."

The fourth Christmas of the war was celebrated as well as possible. Despite recent catches of game, it was not a great success. Most people were utterly tired. Many were half sick. There was a lack of the jubilation that everyone felt should be present. It seemed strange. After all, the campaign was over, wasn't it? The British had won, hadn't they? The Nigerians' 4th Battalion sat down that day with only eight officers who had sat down together for dinner on the previous Christmas. Some of the other battalions had suffered even more from casualties and disease.

On January 12, an evacuation of the Rovuma area was begun. It was decided to continue the campaign, somewhat reluctantly, by once more going down the coast, this time to the Portuguese port of Porto Amelia, and to strike inland, and also to send a column toward von Lettow from Nyasaland.

The few survivors of the 25th Fusiliers, the Nigerians and the Indians were to leave East Africa. The campaign was to be continued by the K.A.R., the West India Regiment, and the Gold Coast Regiment from Porto Amelia, and the Rhodesians and K.A.R. from Nyasaland, together with British and South African staff, the Cape Corps, artillery batteries, the Royal Flying Corps, and various services. A large staff and depot organization would remain at Dar-es-Salaam and Nairobi.

Untroubled from the rear and seldom opposed on its way, the German column marched on. Realizing that he was likely to have little trouble from the British for some time, especially with the rains once more about to come on, von Lettow split his force into two columns, one under General Wahle and the other under himself. The main force attacked and captured three more small Portuguese forts in December, gaining from these minor conquests useful supplies. Enough rations were secured to last the best part of a week each time, by which time it was hoped another Portuguese post would be come upon and captured.

Von Lettow's main trouble was not with the Portuguese,

but with Dr. Schnee. The bespectacled civil servant seemed to infuriate the tough, arrogant soldier. Schnee had insisted on accompanying the column. It was, he said, in accordance with a regulation that the Governor was also military head of the colony. Von Lettow, in his turn, insisted that this certainly did not apply in time of war with a European power, and that anyway they were no longer in the colony. Schnee did his best to interfere with practically every move the soldier made. As the weeks went on bitterness and jealousies increased between the two. It seemed there was no escape, the one from the other, until they should be parted by battle or the war's end—and no one knew how long that would be. At about this time a desperate attempt from Berlin to reach von Lettow with supplies and various experts was made with a Zeppelin, *L.59*, the "Balkan Terror," by Commander von Buttar. It left Bulgaria in November, 1917, but turned back at Khartoum. There was acute disappointment in Berlin at the failure of this dramatic mission to make contact with the last German overseas force still fighting. There is no doubt that the German High Command realized the importance of continuing the campaign, not only from the point of view of the vast expense it was causing the British, but also because of the Allied troops and services being detained in East Africa.

Throughout 1918, Portuguese resistance in P.E.A. was slight. Numerically strong, their army was widely scattered and seldom under effective control. Local commanders usually preferred to flee before von Lettow's advance, or to give in after firing a few token shots. On no occasion did they either destroy their stores before relinquishing their posts, or successfully manage to take them with them. One or two posts, however, now began to put up a stiffer resistance. One lasted out a siege for several days, until its water supply was cut off. Prisoners taken at these posts were usually released, owing to the difficulty of feeding them. At one such post there was embarrassment when the Portuguese commanding officer, having just surrendered, went to pour out a brandy for his German opposite number, only to find the bottle was empty. An askari had got there first. The staple diet at this time was, once more, hippopotamus, which tasted, according to von Lettow, like coarse beef. The lard and tongue of the animal were also much sought after.

At a station of the Portuguese Nyasa Company, the force found a comparatively comfortable resting place and remained there some weeks. There were some large buildings, the first to be found south of the Rovuma, and plantations of fruit trees and vegetables. Carefully laid out roads were fringed by mango and mulberry trees. It was not the last time that the German officers were to be impressed by the neat and productive Portuguese plantations.

Strong patrols and hunting parties were sent out from time to time, but there was little activity. There were no signs of any strong Portuguese force; it seemed, as von Lettow had hoped, that the Portuguese army was split up into hundreds of small units throughout the territory. Questioning of such Africans as they met revealed that native dissatisfaction and latent rebellion was such that the Portuguese found it necessary to patrol their territory ceaselessly. An Italian who had been hunting elephants staggered into the German lines one day, starving and in rags. After some recuperation he offered to join von Lettow's force, but was soon so sick again that he was of little use.

In the second week of January, a British column of two battalions of K.A.R. from Nyasaland was in action against a strong von Lettow patrol, and shortly afterward there was light fighting against the Cape Corps. Both the British probes came to a halt for the time being, but there were many brushes between patrols, and small skirmishes.

At this time a British propaganda campaign was put under way, as a prelude to the engagements that it was hoped would result from the Porto Amelia landings and that would finish with von Lettow once and for all. The askaris were war-weary and longed for their homes. They were in a strange land they had hardly heard of before. The farther they went the less chance there was of ever returning. Propaganda was made by word of mouth through local Africans, and by simple pamphlets. Quite a number of askaris deserted.

The British force proceeding to Porto Amelia was not making rapid progress.

"Pamforce," as the column was known, had embarked at Lindi in December. The main transport ship, the *Salamis,* with most of the force on board, had struck a reef after traveling only a few miles down the coast. Efforts to move her proved unavailing. So did further efforts at the next high tide. Two whalers arrived, but they also failed to move the *Salamis.* After some further delay, it was decided to transfer "Pamforce" to another ship. This difficult operation was accomplished without mishap, whereupon the Porto Amelia expedition steamed back to Lindi—leaving much of its stores and kit behind, most of which the force was never to see again. Some days later two ships made the journey from Lindi to Porto Amelia, a distance of 180 miles, successfully.

Porto Amelia had a depressing effect on the little expeditionary force. A singularly unattractive town, sweltering in oppressive heat, it was the administrative headquarters of the Nyasa Company, which leased northern Mozambique (a province of Portuguese East Africa) from the Portuguese Government. The administration was mainly concerned with the collecting of a poll-tax and a hut-tax which was levied on the inhabitants of the interior, and which was paid in kind. This tax was the main cause of friction between African and Portuguese and accounted for the large number of *bomas* in the hinterland. There was a short pier jutting from a dirty beach, along which ran a row of seedy shops and commercial buildings. These and the native houses crowded behind were almost entirely made of mud, with grass roofs for the Africans and corrugated iron roofs for the Europeans. Only the Governor's house was constructed of concrete and wood. Flies swarmed everywhere and there was a musty smell of animals, human waste, and decaying fruit piled in the ramshackle warehouses, as the troops marched through the narrow lanes towards their camp. Others landed at a beach a few miles from the town.

"Pamforce" had arrived at Porto Amelia by January 7, 1918, with its pioneers and ancillary services. It soon found that it was living in a land of decay. Even outside the town the roads were overgrown, and half-built residences had been left to disintegrate by Europeans who got sick or gave up years before. The one road originally designed for motor traffic, which delved into the interior, was found to be completely overgrown.

During February and March the force hacked its way inland. But the progress was tremendously slow. It was decided by van Deventer to increase the force with two battalions of K.A.R., under Lieutenant-Colonel Giffard. During March there was increasing activity as the column met with German patrols, going farther and farther afield in their search for supplies. "Pamforce," under the command of Brigadier-General Edwards, was now large enough and active enough to cause a real threat to von Lettow. Its progress towards

him, and that of Northey's column from Nyasaland, was slow
but steady.

Realizing that his best plan was to move in a line in the
center of Portuguese territory, thus stretching the supply
lines of the two British forces to their limits and so weaken-
ing their effectiveness, von Lettow decided to move farther
south—on a route as nearly equidistant from the coast and
Nyasaland as possible. His first move took him across the
Lujenda River, in full flood. The whole column was transported across in the only three canoes available. The supply
problem became, as usual when on the move, intense. Von
Lettow, whose hobby was mycology, had been making a
close study of the various mushrooms and fungi to be found
in the area, and he pronounced them fit to eat although somewhat indigestible. He himself enjoyed gathering them in
basketfuls, but he was now down with a severe bout of malaria (a fever to which, he says, he was "particularly sensi-
tive") and was carried along, in a debilitated state, on the
back of a mule. The next headquarters was made at Nanungu, where spirits were greatly heightened by a wireless
message which had at last been received from Germany. It
gave them news of a great German offensive on the Western
Front that, it seemed, was going to win the war for the Fatherland. Von Lettow laid a wager with his senior surgeon
that Amiens would soon fall. The same surgeon, a few days
later, had to remove one of von Lettow's toenails, the toe
having become infected with the jigger-flea. This was not von
Lettow's only personal problem. Besides the three flesh
wounds he had sustained early in the war, a blade of tall
grass had pierced his right eyeball on a recent reconnoitering
expedition. The result of this was that he could no longer

read handwriting or maps, as the left eye had already been injured in the Hottentot Rebellion in German Southwest Africa. "Suitable spectacles could not, however, be obtained and so I was compelled to carry out various enterprises without being able to see properly."

Von Lettow's patrols had reached the coast south of Porto Amelia, where Portuguese ammunition, machine guns, rifles, and—most important—supplies, had been carried off. With his inner position von Lettow was well aware that he could attack either the "Pamforce" or the Nyasa force singly, and this he now contrived to do. The outlying patrols were recalled to Nanungu, and while a large detachment was left to hold up the advance of "Pamforce," he set off with his main force to launch an attack in the west.

The first engagement was behind the main British force from Nyasaland, when one of von Lettow's patrols surprised a fortified supply depot. The Rhodesians, realizing that the stores were lost, fell upon the liquor in the camp and made sure it would not fall into German hands. They were, recorded the German commander, "captured in a thoroughly intoxicated condition."

Northey's force met the Germans head-on and there was some heavy fighting before they withdrew and dug in. Von Lettow, unusually for him since the early days of the campaign, was in the thick of the fighting, smoking away furiously ("It was my habit to smoke continuously during serious fighting"). Fearing for his stores at Nanungu, von Lettow retreated the following night, leaving a detachment to slow up the advance from Nyasaland. Meanwhile, on April 12, 1918, the columns from Porto Amelia had also been engaged, at Medo; during some desperate fighting there were heavy casualties on both sides. At Medo, Dr. Schnee brought von Lettow's wrath upon himself by marching at the head of a column, having attached himself to it during the Commander-in-Chief's absence. He had led it straight into an ambush. A number of askaris were captured, together with 70,000 rounds of ammunition, 30,000 rupees of von Lettow's home-made money and all the Governor's personal possessions. On his return to Nanungu von Lettow showed some generosity of spirit by visiting the dejected Governor and presenting him with "a pair of blue socks, which his wife had made me at the beginning of the war, but which unfortunately had faded."

The German troops were concentrated, Nanungu was evacuated and the great trek continued south. On May 22, 1918, at Korewa, the column just escaped before "Pamforce" and one of Northey's columns from the west (Grifcol) effected a junction. The recent fighting had produced many wounded and it was found that most of these could not be carried fast enough in the litters slung for them between bearers. From time to time they were left in field hospitals, with medical orderlies, in the hope that the pursuing British would come across them. On these occasions, von Lettow spoke to each man separately, shook his hand and wished him luck. Nearly all these discarded wounded and sick, including British prisoners, were found and sent back to Dar-es-Salaam, but there is little doubt that a few of them were never seen again.

Reaching the Lurio River, the German force had to cross to the southern bank hastily as the British were hard behind them, now making successful use of motor transport on the better tracks being found as the chase progressed southwards. The German rear-guard, under Captain Koehl (known as "Cole's Rear-guard" to the British), was sharply engaged on the northern bank of the river by a British force of three battalions.

Von Lettow now changed his tactics for a short time and withdrew in echelon instead of in single column. His intention was to sandwich General Edwards's columns between any two of his own and thus surprise him on the flanks. This ambitious plan did not come off owing to the insuperable difficulties of communication and the strong discipline of the K.A.R. and Gold Coast Regiment, which refused to be panicked. There was, however, an occasional mix-up between columns, with all their bearers and various accoutrements, during which neither side knew who was before them and who behind. Such occasions could be extremely nerve-racking and more than a few died from the bullets of their own countrymen. At this time, too, suicides became more common (the whites, riddled with malaria, had been warned that acute depression is a malarial condition). There were now a number of British columns in the field: Edwards's "Pamforce" of Kartucol (1/2, 2/2 and 3/2 K.A.R. under Colonel Giffard) and Rosecol (Gold Coast Regiment and K.A.R. under Colonel Rose); Kartrecol (3rd K.A.R.); Shortcol (K.A.R. and Rhodesian Native Regiment under Colonel Shorthose—commonly known as "Soxcol"); Grifcol (K.A.R. from Nyasaland); and, later, Fitzcol (K.A.R.) and Mobforce (from Mozambique).

Von Lettow was still meeting but little resistance from the Portuguese. The situation was summed up by one of his older officers, a South African Boer: "This is a funny war. We chase the Portuguese and the English chase us." A more settled part of Portuguese East Africa was now being entered. The local forts provided more comfort and better stores. At one, the head of the German column surprised the Portuguese officers and N.C.O.s drinking coffee on the veranda of a fine, extensive house. Plantations had large European houses and supplies were captured with frequency at the Portuguese posts, which had been conveniently built a day's march from each other. Orange trees were in bloom. Pigs were even found and sausages made (the first enjoyment of this luxury was such that von Lettow's officers refused to be disturbed even when shots from a British advance party fell in their camp). The possibilities of indiscriminate looting were obvious and von Lettow, while only too glad to grab every supply he could, found time to "point out the evils of such behavior."

No one knew exactly where they were heading. The next big obstacle was the Zambezi itself. After that? Well, Salisbury would only be 300 miles away. And they had covered more than that from the Rovuma already.

The trek continued along little-known native tracks, or even right through the bush, often in single file. Owing to the great length of the column, once more a single unit, the head had to start off in the dark, at about 5 a.m., if the tail was to reach the next camp before dark the same day. Even on arrival, there was much work to be done at the end of the day in setting up camp, providing shelters for the sick and in administration and paperwork, which von Lettow meticulously kept up, including charges and daily details. Yet another river, the Likungo, was crossed; 400 yards wide, it came up to the necks of the shortest and took about an hour for each person to cross.

A railway line near Quelimane was reached. Passengers on a train puffing up from the coast were astonished to find German troops holding up the way. On July 1–3, 1918, a heavy fight took place at a large plantation, depot and railway station, called Nhamacurra, and over 100 infantry of the K.A.R. were drowned in a neighboring river while fleeing from a fierce German charge. Two companies of K.A.R., a total of

300 men, suffered 223 casualties and missing. Von Lettow claimed the following British losses, not taking into account those lost by drowning: 100 K.A.R. and four British officers killed; 421 K.A.R. and Portuguese native troops, five British officers and 117 Portuguese European troops taken prisoner. He made one of his best hauls of captured stores. The head of supply was "in despair" at finding ways of carrying away such booty—including 300,000 kilograms of food, enough clothing for all the askaris to take as much as they wanted, 350 British and Portuguese rifles and ten machine guns. Some light guns had been rendered useless, but one was reconstructed by using the serviceable parts of three guns. The German column had, in fact, stumbled on one of the main supply depots of the Allies in Portuguese East Africa. It was not found possible to take away the whole stock of wine that had also been captured and von Lettow allowed everyone to let himself go for once. There were also a large number of casks of spirits. "With the best will in the world it was impossible to drink it all," von Lettow has said, and the dregs had to be poured away into the river. To add to the embarrassments of the chief of supply, shortly after the capture of the depot a river steamer arrived. A British officer disembarked, all unsuspecting of what had happened, and on board were found more than 300 cases of cartridges.

Von Lettow decided to change his plan. He was not far from the important port of Quelimane, having bypassed the other main port of the area, Mozambique. He realized that the Allies would be mounting stiff defences there, especially after the defeat he had recently inflicted on the strong advance outpost and supply depot, and that the forces behind him would be speeding up their pursuit. The main route to Quelimane lay along a parallel route to his own and he suspected that the pursuing columns would take this in order to reach the port first. So von Lettow decided to remain where he was for the while, resting his troops, tending to the sick and enjoying the newly-won supplies. Then, when the British force had overshot the mark, he intended to reverse his direction and march north.

The main problem of the British force was, as always, one of its ever-lengthening supply line. The farther the Germans went the less fit were the British to attack them successfully and bring the whole affair to an end. Von Lettow's rearguard, waiting around corners, behind rocks and in clumps of trees, heavily armed with machine guns, had a nasty sting. Officers and men were mentally and physically revolted by the continual marching, day after day, week after week; chasing a foe that never stopped long enough to give serious battle. German patrols, operating far behind the rear of the British columns, occasionally came across their supplies and, even more infuriating, their mails. Most of the British would rather have given up their rations for forty-eight hours than their precious, longed-for mails which reminded them of a world that seemed to exist in another universe. (A German diary revealed that such a bag of captured mails contained only love notes and information as to the state of gardens at home, and nothing of the state of the war on the Western Front about which the diarist longed to know.) The British supply line was now 168 miles from Porto Amelia. British troops were also being sent to Mozambique and Quelimane, and sent inland. Von Lettow had met some of these already. From Lake Nyasa two small columns and one which had come all the way from the Rovuma, under Northey's command, were still in the hunt. In June, 1918, Northey went on leave prior to becoming Governor of British East Africa. His command was taken over by Brigadier-General G. M. P.

Hawthorn, who had started the war as a major in B.E.A. The Gold Coast Regiment, completely worn out, having campaigned ceaselessly since its arrival in East Africa in July, 1916, was withdrawn. It had arrived 1,428 strong. Several drafts had arrived since then, but when it left it had to record 1,790 casualties and invalided, including nearly 1,000 killed or wounded in action. These figures well indicate the severity of the fighting when German and British columns met in brief but bloody clashes. (In August, 1917, there had been 245 army doctors with the force; it was estimated that 450 were required.)

A mounted column had been formed from the Gold Coast Regiment to operate in the open bush wherever the opportunity arose. Four riding schools had been constructed near Porto Amelia and 170 men trained as mounted infantry. They proved to be useful for scouting purposes. They would go off with three days' rations and one blanket each and often discover the exact whereabouts of von Lettow's troops. A number of them were captured but made a daring escape. They remained in operation in East Africa after the rest of the regiment had left for home. Another mounted unit were the KARMI (K.A.R. Mounted Infantry).

Thomas Muir, an R.E. (Royal Engineers) signalman attached to one of the "Pamforce" columns from Porto Amelia (known as "Portamelia" to the British force) has described the typical formation and conditions of British columns in Portuguese East. "The battalions took daily turn about leading and the companies rotated as to which provided the screen. The very first point was a single askari, a few paces behind him two askaris, a few paces behind them the screen consisting of a company at about two yards between men. At the center of that, connecting files of pairs and then in marching formation the remaining companies of the battalion, with the colonel of the leading battalion at their head and near him Signals running out its wire. Then more connecting files to the second battalion with Signals making the wire safe. All these people had ammo porters and what we called first-line equipment, i.e. material that was required far actual fighting. Second-line loads followed the second battalion. These loads were of daily needs such as food, essential but not fighting stuff. The third battalion's job was to round-up stragglers and provide a rear-guard. Third-line loads included spare stores, ambulance, spare kit and so on. The whole travelled at the slow pace set by the load-carrying porters. At night, when perimeter was formed once it had been decided which battalion was on duty, the position of any unit was always relatively the same as before and could readily be found.

"We often went on for days with no sign of Gerry. Then our scouts would get information and off we'd rush at forced march pace, everyone tired and hungry and especially thirsty. Gerry being in advance knew where the water was and operated accordingly. He would tempt us off the water holes and then defend the next one fiercely. When it suited him, he retired. We had to go warily to avoid traps and then when it was clear he was well away, we'd have the same mad rush again. It was almost a relief to know we had made definite contact as it was always pretty nervy wondering where Gerry was and when he was going to open fire.

"When a column moved off on a new stunt, say from the coast, the porter supply was fairly tight but as food was eaten and ammo shot off, porters became available for all sorts of jobs. We each reckoned to have three personal porters, one to carry the bedding-clothing load, one for the food load and one for our equipment. We carried nothing whatever ourselves

when we were not within touch of Gerry. Our sun helmets
went on to the boy's head the minute the sun went down and
we donned our soft caps.

"Flies were much more disliked than mosquitoes. Tsetse
were the worst of all. There was a brute with a proboscis like
a bayonet who could even pierce puttees. A dead body at-
tracted flies within less than an hour in such numbers that
their damned wings made a sound like water falling. If there
was time, stones were always put on top to keep the jackals
out. I once came on to the column at nightfall and was scared
stiff to see blokes climbing out of graves. Actually there had
been no stones and the jackals had pulled them out. When a
donkey was attacked by tsetse his head swelled until he could
not hold it up. He was then taken into the bush and shot.

"It's funny but we in a subconscious sort of way thought
of Gerry as another bunch of unfortunates like ourselves,
only on the wrong side.

"At Medo our medical arrangements consisted of one Indian surgeon and stretcher bearers. One chap told me that
when he had been dressing wounded there was no water to
wash his blood-soaked arms and he had to spend his time
rubbing off the ants that crawled up his bloody arms like ink
on blotting paper.

"I only saw white, or rather fresh, bread at Dar-es-Salaam
and then it was made with Indian flour. We sometimes had
flour on the column and then we tried our heavy hand at
making bread with sour dough as rising agent. Apart from
that, the ration was supposed to be six hard biscuits, 1 lb.
bully, 2 oz. Ideal Milk, and odd stuff like coffee and tobacco
per day. In practice, on the column, we seemed just to share
what we had when we had it. Sometimes tins of jam came up.
I never saw a tea issue. We bought that at the coast ourselves
—using old German East coins and von Lettow's paper notes.

We even got paid in German money. Native rations seemed to consist of mealie-meal, dates, rice and salt. Favored boys occasionally had bully from us when plenty was about. We also had meat on hoof when it managed to join us.

"On one occasion, we had a message from the Base that as we were moving into thickly populated country, American cloth was being sent up in lieu of rations. We should use that for trading. We then marched into a desert and Gerry in front of us had gleaned off everything edible. Our ammo at that time was being carried partly on donkeys in netting panniers. We sent back a famous message saying we had killed and eaten our donkeys and were now immobile. I was lucky in that I was running a fever at the time and so was not eating. Another time a consignment of pliers was sent up. Most of us had them already, so we did not want them. But they insisted. We took them and threw them away into the bush. When I was invalided back to Dar-es-Salaam, I just could not see what all that crowd could find to do to arrange things for the few of us on column. Von Lettow was reported to have said that we had more staff officers at Dar-es than he had white men in the colony."

Von Lettow started to move northeast in July, 1918. Information from his patrols told him that an extraordinary situation was taking place. British columns, from Porto Amelia and the north, and from the Lake Nyasa area, were marching south and southwest, while he was marching between them in the opposite direction.

He now had quite a large number of European prisoners that he had collected in recent months. He was less willing to release them than before; Portuguese officers had been released on giving their word they would not fight him again in the war, only to be discovered later doing just that. Von

Lettow noticed that the British prisoners took the hardships of the march without complaint, but that the Portuguese were forever protesting about the quality and scarcity of the food and the frequent uncomfortable fording of rivers. "For the most part they were infected with syphilis . . . and they were not real campaigners," he said.

It was inevitable that sooner or later the German column should meet one of the British columns lagging behind its partners and this happened at Namirrue on July 22. The column concerned was one of Hawthorn's. Von Lettow sent a detachment round to its rear, and the German commanding this unit was startled to hear the barking of a dog while maneuvering his men into position. On investigating, he found the British commanding officer, a Lieutenant-Colonel Dickinson, telephoning in a ravine. He was with his dog, adjutant and medical officer. They were all taken prisoner. Part of the British force was overwhelmed, and withdrew. The remainder were entrenched in a strong position on the crown of a hill. A trench mortar, with ammunition, had been captured by the Germans. Some hasty practice was made with it, to see how it worked, and it was then trained on to the British trenches. On the hill were the Gold Coast Mounted Infantry. The mortar kept up an accurate fire and practically every member of the mounted detachment was killed, as well as all their horses, before they raised the white flag. This meant that nearly the whole of one of Hawthorn's columns had been wiped out and the way northwest, towards Lake Nyasa and the Rovuma, or—and von Lettow was considering such a course—west towards Blantyre in Nyasaland, was practically clear. Only one other sizeable British force remained in the way. Giffard's Kartucol, by now legendary in East Africa, arrived at Namirrue a day too late, having marched 300 miles, practically without rations and with no blankets or kit.

In this engagement a number of K.A.R. that had been recruited from captured German askaris were taken prisoner. They now reverted to their original role. Shortly afterward von Lettow received a message from van Deventer asking for an exchange of medical prisoners and requesting permission to supply the British prisoners with food. He wanted to know where such supplies could be handed over. But von Lettow, quite unjustifiably, suspected a trap and marched on. He was soon harried by small British columns, who, at last, had broken away from their clumsy supply lines and were living light and off the land, as the Germans themselves did whenever a Portuguese depot was not at hand. One of the chasing units was a force of South African motorcyclists. They split into two detachments and shot at each other with tragic results. There was a brief engagement at Namarroe on August 24, 1918, in which the Germans lost more casualties than they had for some weeks. Von Lettow called off an attempt to take a British depot, heavily guarded, and decided to hurry towards the east of Lake Nyasa, abandoning any idea of marching west into Nyasaland. He guessed that a thrust north toward German East would seem to have as its obvious objective the rail town of Tabora, and that the British would, accordingly, withdraw their troops from Portuguese East Africa by sea to Dar-es-Salaam and then take rail for Tabora. In this way he might get some respite and could, at the last moment, veer away from Tabora and not attempt to take it at all. In the event, his expectations were very largely realized.

The march north was a long and tedious affair. No guides could be found. The country was only partly explored and was entirely unknown to the Germans. Von Lettow could only give general instructions to the commander of his advance party, pointing at some hills, or vaguely across the bush. The long column wound its way back across the wilderness, over the Lurio once more and then on towards the Rovuma. As the crow flew, there were 250 miles to go before the ex-German colony was reached. As bare feet and disintegrating boots marched, no one knew how far it would be or how long it would take.

Once more, all the wounded and sick, including sick prisoners, were left behind, this time in charge of a British army doctor. There was another stiff engagement with a small column of Hawthorn's which put up a bitter fight and which caused him ninety-five German casualties. On this occasion the Germans also lost 48,000 rounds of ammunition, important medical stores and a part of the traveling arsenal including many rifle-parts. Three battalions of K.A.R. took part in this engagement and their losses were also heavy. At one moment victory had seemed near for the British at last, when the Germans had been separated—one section under Wahle and the other under von Lettow. The two were reunited only after von Lettow's section, porters, women and askaris, had scrambled down a steep escarpment, slipping and stumbling on loose stones. Those who had boots were forced to remove them, and some to leave them behind, in order to get down.

After these two desperate little battles, the way to the Rovuma was clear. Picking up its loads for two hours at a time, singing sadly as it went, then laying down the loads for an hour's rest, the column moved on. But an enemy as dangerous as the British now suddenly fell on the force. It seemed to come from nowhere. One day it had not been there; the next day it was everywhere. It was influenza. Soon about half were down with it, or with bronchial catarrh. It was only possible for eighty men to be carried at any one time, so many of the sick had to march. There was no solution to the problem, short of abandoning the campaign, as von Lettow would not leave the sick to die in the bush. He ordered them to get up and march. Nevertheless, as the days went on an increasing number of askaris and other Africans gradually fell behind. At night they arrived late in camp. Then, one night, they did not arrive at all.

They now entered a rich and lush countryside. Natives were met with once more. Some of them had seldom, if ever, seen a white man before. Game was everywhere. The Rovuma could not be far off. Weak and sick, the German army in Africa, having shaken off its pursuers far behind, staggered on. Sentries were so weak and exhausted at night that they hardly put up any resistance when carried away by lions. Every day the sick were dying of influenza.

There was little feeling of triumph when the gently-flowing Rovuma, muddy and languid-looking, was sighted on September 28, 1918.

Chapter 12

THE DELAYED ARMISTICE

During the campaign in Portuguese East Africa, a large staff organization and auxiliary services had been growing every month at British bases from Porto Amelia as far back as Nairobi. Officers and the N.C.O.s were continually being drafted to the campaign from the Western Front. On the ships out, some of them boasted of how they had managed to "wangle" their postings to East Africa, which certainly sounded, by all accounts, a more pleasant war than the wretchedness of Flanders and France. Those newly arrived in 1918 were surprised to find German civilians wandering around in Dar-es-Salaam and Tanga, going about their normal business. One recorded of Dar-es-Salaam, where van Deventer still had his headquarters, "The staff was very much in evidence, and it must have been a very large staff indeed to judge by the number of red-tabbed field officers to be met with everywhere.

Not even at Army Headquarters in France had I ever seen so many red tabs and decorations." To keep the few columns in the field it was apparently necessary to keep these centers, such as Dar-es-Salaam, Lindi and Kilwa, far distant from the fighting, full of staff officers and clerks. An army, however small, cannot fight without them. It needs its supplies, its pay, its doctors and its instructions. It also needs its replacements, and for this purpose a K.A.R. training depot had been set up at Nairobi, to which officers and N.C.O.s from Europe were posted. Training was interrupted now and again, as when a battalion of K.A.R. threatened mutiny and had to be disarmed, and during an expedition against the Masai. This latter was an affair the officers from Europe did not enjoy. A "punitive expedition," it consisted of firing machine guns on half-naked warriors in ostrich feather headdresses, who attempted to protect themselves behind buffalo-hide shields. None got near enough to the machine-gunners and riflemen to use their spears.

One of the biggest surprises for those from the trenches was their first meeting with Sergeant Oosterhuizen at the Nairobi depot. He wore on his tunic the South African War campaign ribbons. On being questioned about this he explained that another sergeant instructor of the depot, of the Leicestershire Regiment, also wore them, and as he had fought in the same battles he just could not see why he should not wear them also—even if he had fought on the other side. No one was able to dissuade him. Somehow, his logic seemed as good as theirs.

In German East once more, von Lettow came on "amazingly" fertile country. He surprised one or two depots and small columns which had received no warning of his approach and he slowed down the pace of the march, his force returning to near-complete fitness. At the small town of Songea the advance party, as usual a day's march ahead, came across stiff opposition from mortars and entrenched infantry. At this time, van Deventer was rushing troops up the railway as fast as they could go to protect Tabora, the railway itself, and the Rhodesian frontier, and forestall the possibility of an attack farther north towards Lake Tanganyika. Proper trains were in use once more and they clattered furiously up the line, packed with troops from bases at Dar-es-Salaam and Lindi, and those newly returned from Portuguese East Africa.

In October, 1918, the world at large, which had long since forgotten about the German East campaign, was astonished to hear of a strong German column advancing on Tabora and threatening British territory.

As von Lettow progressed, a number of his carriers deserted and even some of the askaris. After so many months away they wanted only to go to their homes, which were not far distant. Some of them, including one of von Lettow's personal servants, returned after a few days' "leave." Besides the increasing opposition in front, there was also a strong column on his heels, which had almost caught up with him. The German rear-guard was severely attacked. Von Lettow realized that the time had come to veer off sharply to the west and enter Rhodesia, while the British still concentrated on their feverish efforts to protect the Central Railway. This he now did, on October 17, leaving several sick and wounded behind, including General Wahle, who at last gave up the struggle with sickness after campaigning for four years in a war that he, a retired General, had stumbled into by accident.

This district was little known to the German force, being a remote corner of their former colony, and those few who did know it found it much changed, with new roads and forts constructed by the British occupying troops. At one of these forts, captured by von Lettow, the Germans learned from newspapers they found there of the collapse of their troops on the Western Front and of Haig's Last Push. The papers were over three weeks old, but they learned of the fall of Cambrai, St. Quentin and Armentières.

Von Lettow sent his patrols out far and wide, some nearly as far as Lake Tanganyika, and another was already in Rhodesian territory near the township of Fife. A race took place between a strong column of K.A.R. and von Lettow's column to reach Fife first. Von Lettow had no exact knowledge of where Fife was, but his force "advanced along a mountain ridge on to a point where we judged that Fife would be." The ground was covered with knee-high grass. A tremendous strain was put on the German column by a ten-hour march, but when they got there the British had already arrived in the form of a detachment of Northern Rhodesian Police. Well entrenched on the outskirts, this small force beat off the very much greater numbers of the German force after two days' fighting. They were outnumbered by at least ten to one. The police were supported by the hastily armed civilian population. Here von Lettow's trench mortar was destroyed by a premature burst. He moved off with his soldiers, the sun gleaming on the barrels of their rifles, the women in their gay colors, his patient bearers who squatted behind the lines when fighting was in progress, and his herd of over 400 cattle. A nearby mission station and hospital were found evacuated. Here he acquired enough quinine to last until June, 1919. The next important township was Kasama, 100 miles to the southwest. The German column followed the well-marked road. Small advance parties were hurried on to scout out the land, then followed the strong advance-guard, with the main body a day's march behind. Behind all was the rear-guard, fighting nearly every day the British force of K.A.R. (750 rifles guided by a local settler) which could do nothing but follow wherever von Lettow wished to lead it. The K.A.R. commander had only a small atlas of the world, 200 miles to the inch.

There were hardly any other British troops in the area, the Rhodesian forces not yet having returned from Portuguese territory across Lake Nyasa, and the vast bulk of the British forces still around the Central Railway, some hundreds of miles to the rear. Where was von Lettow heading? That was the question that intrigued and worried civil servants and local commanders for 500 miles around. Some said he intended to cut across Africa to the ex-German territory of South-West Africa. Others said he was heading for Angola. Whatever he did, it was certain that there was practically nothing strong enough to stop him while he marched south toward Salisbury and Bulawayo. Von Lettow himself had only a vague idea of where he was heading—south toward lands rich in supplies and food, as yet untouched by war, where there would be, he suspected, nothing stronger than local police forces to stop him.

A Catholic missionary station was passed, consisting of "wonderful, spacious and massive buildings." After nearly two years in the wilderness it was an excitement to be reminded of civilization. The missionaries had fled. Von Lettow was annoyed by this, considering it quite unnecessary. He was also annoyed by a letter left him by a nun, appealing to his humanity; it especially irritated him because she was, like himself, a native of Westphalia. The whole countryside was in terror of the German advance, believing all the unfounded rumors of atrocities that abounded. Kasama was taken on November 9, the garrison, only half a company strong and consisting mainly of wayward African troops, hurriedly released from jail, having retreated southward. The evacuation of Kasama had been almost complete. Porters had run away, but somehow the inhabitants, using every means available, had managed to make off with some of the stores. All native villages near the line of German advance had also been ordered to be evacuated. Von Lettow was as impressed with the house of the District Commissioner, "furnished with great taste," as he was with the haul of ammunition and supplies. The farther the column went from Fife the more and fuller the depots that the marchers came across. Von Lettow decided to push on to the Chambezi River.

On November 11, von Lettow cycled up to his advance-guard to discuss the situation with its commander. It was a fine day, sunny but not too hot. After a short conference, the march was continued, everyone feeling more confident than for many months. There seemed no reason why most of Rhodesia should not be put to havoc. Far away, across mountains, jungles, the deserts of North Africa, and the sea, millions were rejoicing in the streets and shouting from windows, at the end of the most terrible war man had ever known. In New York and Brussels, in London and Paris, there was only one word that could consistently be heard above the din—"Armistice." The war was over. There was to be peace and good will on earth forevermore.

There could have been only a few dozen in all those millions who knew anything of Clause Seventeen of the Armistice signed that morning by Germany. This provided for unconditional surrender of all German forces operating in East Africa within one month from November 11, it being thought that the terms of the Armistice might take some time to reach the German force in that theater, still active in the field.

On November 12, there was heavy fighting between the rear-guard and the British column, which had surprised the

Germans by not following directly and by taking a parallel course. The tired force of British-led K.A.R., knowing nothing of the Armistice, nearly inflicted a serious defeat on some of von Lettow's strongest companies. The heavy rifle and machine-gun fire could be clearly heard all that night from the camp of the main German body.

On November 13, the German advance party reached the Chambezi River. Von Lettow was selecting a site for a camp when one of his officers rode up on a bicycle and told him that a British motorcyclist had arrived with the news of an Armistice. He had brought a telegram which read, "To be forwarded via M.B. cable and dispatch-rider. Send following to Colonel von Lettow-Vorbeck under white flag. The Prime Minister of England has announced that an Armistice was signed at five hours on Nov 11 and that hostilities on all fronts cease at eleven hours on Nov 11 stop I am ordering my troops to cease hostilities forthwith unless attacked and of course I conclude that you will do the same stop Conditions of Armistice will be forwarded you immediately I receive them stop Meanwhile I suggest you should remain in your present vicinity in order to facilitate communication— General van Deventer."

Von Lettow went on bicycle to his advance-guard, forty miles away on the northern bank of the Chambezi, which was being faced by a small British force on the opposite bank. He immediately made plans for crossing the river, in case "hostilities were resumed." Another cable from van Deventer reached him that night after he had gone to bed in the local German commander's tent. It was couched in stronger terms, demanding immediate surrender of all British prisoners of war, and ordered von Lettow to march his column north to Abercorn forthwith in order to lay down arms. Van Deventer added, "I will, however, allow you and your officers and European other ranks to retain their personal weapons for the present in consideration of the gallant fight you have made."

The following day, von Lettow, still unwilling to believe in the total collapse of Germany, handed to a British liaison officer a telegram for the Kaiser,* reporting what had happened, to make sure that by surrendering he was doing the correct thing. He received no reply. Before the prisoners were released the most senior of them, Colonel Dickinson, came to say good-bye on their behalf.

The return march began, through Kasama, to Abercorn. There was some difficulty with the askaris. They did not wish to lay down their arms and at first made it clear that when they reached Abercorn they would not do so. They wanted to take their rifles and ammunition home. There were not sufficient British troops on the spot to enforce the surrender of arms and the British were forced to ask von Lettow for help. He finally persuaded his men to deliver up their arms. The askaris were also anxious for their pay. This was some years overdue. The same applied to the carriers. The sum involved was one and a half million rupees and von Lettow sent an officer off on a bicycle to get this money from the British. It was not forthcoming. The predicament was unpleasant and could have led to mutiny. Von Lettow sent off a cable to the German Government in Berlin. Once again he received no reply. In the end he carefully drew up lists of all the back pay that was due and gave each carrier and askari a certificate against it. Von Lettow took some interest in this matter after the war, and the certificates were all honored by a German government mission to Tanganyika.

* "To Majestat, Berlin. General Deventer theilt offiziell mit dass nach den von Deutschland unterzeichneten waffenstillstandbedingungen bedingungslose ubergabe der schutztruppen zu erfolgen hat; ich werde entsprechend verfahren. Lettow."

THE DELAYED ARMISTICE

At Kasama the Germans were met by the 1/4 K.A.R., who had recently fought such a fierce engagement with their rear-guard. Their commanding officer, Lieutenant-Colonel E. B. B. Hawkins (a lieutenant at the start of the war—von Lettow was astonished to discover he was hardly in his thirties), asked all the German officers round for lunch. The Germans felt they had to refuse, although they "appreciated such an expression of chivalry." But Colonel Dickinson paid a visit to von Lettow and the two officers had a pleasant hour over a cup of coffee. Hawkins's column was drastically short of supplies and von Lettow had to help him out with cattle. Hawkins later wrote in *The Times* of von Lettow, "Instead of the haughty Prussian one expected to meet, he turned out to be a most courteous and perfectly mannered man."

General Edwards, who had chased von Lettow all the way from Porto Amelia, via Tabora, sent a car for the German commander and he and his staff met von Lettow on arrival in Abercorn. It was near here that, over four years before, the Germans had made their first tentative raids across the Rhodesian border within a month of the outbreak of war. The surrender was formally enacted before many British inhabitants and African troops who had suffered from those early raids. It took place in the square of Abercorn, surrounded by the white, wooden buildings of the town. A flagstaff was erected on some open ground opposite the government offices and at twelve noon on November 25, General Edwards accepted the surrender of Colonel von Lettow-Vorbeck. "Von Lettow, whose striking presence is a good index of what must be a wonderful personality, came in at the head of his first detachment, which consisted of some Europeans, closely followed by some 400 askaris with their machine guns, carriers, medical unit and women. After these troops had quickly formed into three lines in close formation, von Lettow advanced a few paces, saluted the Union Jack, then, taking out a pocket-book, read therefrom his formal statement of surrender in German. He repeated it in English, whereupon General Edwards replied, accepting his surrender on behalf of His Majesty King George V [*Bulawayo Chronicle*]." Von Lettow was then presented to the numerous officers present and afterwards introduced his own, and also Governor Schnee. He was dressed in a rather battered sun helmet covered with corduroy, a bush shirt, corduroy shorts, gray puttees, no badges of rank, and captured boots slit over the toes to make them fit. Several British officers asked permission to photograph him. One of the British officers said, "We had more esteem and affection for him than our own leaders." There followed a dramatic moment in the proceedings, when the German Commander-in-Chief called on his askaris to lay down their arms. Much to everyone's relief, this they did without fuss, piling their rifles and discarding their equipment. They were then led off to an internment camp surrounded by a thorn hedge a mile outside the town.

It started to rain. It was some hours before the arrival and laying down of arms of the whole German force was complete. The Africans from the outlying villages of Abercorn had come in to watch. They stood silently and observed with care the stiff ceremony of the white men, who were so unlike themselves. Some may have even wondered, as they watched, whether the white man would always be there, with his guns, his flags and his hymns.

There are some contradictions as to the exact statistics of the German surrender, but the reporter of the *Bulawayo Chronicle* was possibly the least biased. He gave the following particulars: thirty officers, 125 other Europeans, including five doctors, a veterinary surgeon, a chemist and a signals officer; 1,165 askaris; 1,516 porters; 482 Portuguese bearers; 295 followers and cattle tenders; 819 women. There were also thirty-eight machine guns, one field gun and nearly a quarter of a million rounds of ammunition. "It was a most impressive spectacle. The long motley column, Europeans and askari, all veterans of a hundred fights, the askari clothed with every kind of headgear, women who had stuck to their husbands through all these years of hardships, carrying huge loads, some with children born during the campaign, carriers coming in singing in undisguised joy at the thought that their labors were ended at last."

The war was over. Von Lettow had, employed against him, an army of at least 130,000, together with many senior commanders. He had caused an expenditure by the British alone of £72,000,000, to say nothing of that incurred by Portugal and Belgium. As the British *Official History* says, "He had successfully contained in Africa for over four years a force considerably larger than Lord Roberts's whole army in the South African War." The campaign had cost Britain, according to Cranworth's account, "more money and three times as many lives, if deaths from disease involving porters as well as combatants are included, than did the whole South African War." As for the British and their colonial troops, they had fought one of the most depressing of campaigns, following an elusive enemy, never giving up despite hardships through disease, starvation and distances that at times must have seemed insuperable. Most of them summoned up this courage in a land they had never seen before and that had previously meant little to them. The official British casualty figures were 62,220 (not including those admitted to hospitals through disease), of whom 48,328 died from disease, mostly malaria. These do not include the many thousands of deaths among the carriers. The largest British force engaged were the twenty-two battalions of the

K.A.R., which had a total strength of 35,424 on November 1, 1918, of whom one in nine were Europeans. Their casualties were 8,225. British officers serving with the K.A.R. suffered 22.6 per cent casualties; two-thirds of them were classed as "died of disease." The proportion of deaths to wounded and prisoners in the casualty figures was very much higher in the East African theater than in other fronts of the First World War.

In a dispatch earlier in the war, General Smuts had written, "The plain tale of their achievements bears the most convincing testimony to the spirit, determination, and prodigious efforts of all ranks. Their work has been done under tropical conditions which not only produce bodily weariness and unfitness, but which create mental languor and depression and finally appal the stoutest hearts. To march day by day and week by week through the African jungle or high grass, in which vision is limited to a few yards, in which danger always lurks near but seldom becomes visible, even when experienced, supplies a test to human nature often in the long run beyond the limits of human endurance . . . the strain on all has been overwhelming." Neither Smuts nor anyone else was to know that only twenty-four years later there would be still worse jungle fighting to be done.

Chapter 13

AFTERWARD

All over East Africa a vast migration took place as men made their ways home. Portuguese and Belgians crowded their own ports. The K.A.R. were dispatched all over the area to their depots before disbandment. The 2nd K.A.R. went from Nairobi to Nyasaland, its home country, via Beira in Portuguese East Africa, picking up the 3rd Battalion on the way. It took two months to complete the journey and not until it was completed did the British officers themselves become redundant. A berth in a ship home was the most precious possession a man could have. The German askaris were taken to a camp at Tabora, where they languished for a month and a half before release. The Europeans were taken by boat up Lake Tanganyika to the railhead at Kigoma. At that port the Belgians had prepared tables covered with cloths for them, a sight they had not seen for years. They were feasted and well supplied with red wine. Crowds of Germans and British greeted the prisoners-of-war as the train reached first Tabora, and then Morogoro. At Morogoro the women who had been left behind long before were out on the platform to embrace their menfolk. British and Germans got drunk together. It had been a long war.

At Dar-es-Salaam, Schnee and von Lettow were entertained to lunch by van Deventer. There was great interest in the German commander; everyone was anxious to see him. He was described by one who did as "a tall, spare, square-shouldered man, with close-cropped grey hair and a clear eye which looked you straight in the face." There was some surprise at his perfect command of English.

Influenza broke out over the whole territory, far worse than earlier in the year. Hospitals were as full as they had been during the bitterest fighting. Many British officers, who had survived the whole campaign, died of it in Dar-es-Salaam. In the German internment camps it spread like fire. Ten per cent of the surviving German officers, who had fought in and tramped through the bush for three years, died of influenza in a few weeks. Embarkation of the remaining German troops took place on January 17, 1919. It was five years to the day since von Lettow had arrived at the same port to take up his command. Many of the British survivors did not manage to get home until long after that; when they did they were frequently congratulated by friends on having "missed" the war.

On his return to Germany von Lettow had some momentary glory. He was made a general and given command of a division of the Reichswehr which bore his name. At a campaign dinner held in London, attended by Smuts, he was the guest of honor. He helped to suppress a rebellion of Communists in Hamburg in 1919, but, increasingly involved in politics, he left the army in 1920 when he was only fifty years old. He became a deputy in the Reichstag till 1930, but, disillusioned with political life, he retired to local affairs in Bremen. In 1935, Meinertzhagen, who had become friendly with von Lettow, suggested to Hitler that von Lettow should be made Ambassador in London. "Hitler was a bit astonished, thought a while in silence, then slapped his thigh and thought it a good idea," but von Lettow "loathes Hitler and everything he stands for." The matter was dropped. In the 1930s Hitler said he would one day return the former German colony in East Africa to the Reich. A number of Germans began settling in the territory, to join those who had remained to live under British rule. They were quickly interned in September, 1939. During the last war von Lettow lived in Berlin, but afterwards, almost a forgotten figure, he returned to Bremen, where he received food parcels from Smuts, with whom he corresponded regularly. All his sons were killed in the war, but his two daughters married two brothers. Some years ago he returned on a visit to Tanganyika, and was vociferously received by wildly cheering natives to whom he had become a legendary figure in his own lifetime. But as the years went on and another age came, he lost his former fame and even his proud entry in *Encyclopaedia Britannica* between Lettish Literature and Lettres de Cachet. An official high-school history book * in Tanganyika describes him as dead. He now lives in a suburb of Hamburg and, although well into his nineties, still goes out shooting.

Van Deventer left for South Africa on January 13, 1919, having made arrangements for the garrisoning of the territory—thenceforth to be known as Tanganyika. Knighted after the war, he died in 1922. Northey remained as Gover-

* *A Short History of Tanganyika*, P.H.C. Clarke (Longmans, 1960).

nor of Kenya (formerly British East Africa) till 1922, when he retired to Berkshire. He died in 1953. Colonel Giffard (the fame of his Kartucol spread far and wide) is now General Sir George Giffard; he was C.-in-C. 11th Army Group in Southeast Asia, 1943. The amiable Wapshare, like Tighe, served in the Afghan War of 1919 before he retired. Aitken fought for years to clear his name of the Tanga affair. He was reduced to the rank of colonel and relegated to unemployment on half pay. Eventually he achieved a public statement in Parliament exonerating him from personal blame. He was allowed to retire, a bitter man, with the full retired pay of a colonel, and died in 1924. Lord Cranworth, whose views on the value of the K.A.R. as opposed to white troops were so completely vindicated, lives in Suffolk. General Smuts, on arrival in London in 1917, became a powerful figure in Whitehall and Westminster. In the same year he ended a critical strike in the Welsh coalfields and gave his support to the Passchendaele offensive. He soon became respected as an international statesman. In 1918, he suggested that he should command the American forces in France, a suggestion that never reached President Wilson. He helped in organizing the new R.A.F. He returned to South Africa, where much of the remainder of his life was devoted to furthering the British Commonwealth and the League of Nations, and to keeping Afrikaner nationalists from power. Although his reputation must have suffered if he had commanded in the East African campaign until its conclusion, it is certain that his ambitions and ability would have overcome any setback. He suffered from malaria contracted in German East for the rest of his life.

Meinertzhagen left the War Office after a short spell and was sent to Palestine to serve under Allenby as Intelligence officer. He became friendly with T. E. Lawrence and worked with him. He later became an expert on the Middle East in the Colonial Office and was Chief Political Officer in Palestine. In 1919, he was a member of the Paris Peace Conference. There he met Lloyd George, who wrote of him in his *War Memoirs*, "He struck me as one of the ablest and most successful brains I had met in any army. That was quite sufficient to make him suspect and to hinder his promotion to the higher ranks." In 1923, he was offered the Governorship of the Falkland Islands, which he turned down. He resigned from the army in India in 1925, "gripped by the deadening effect of rules, regulations and a complete absence of responsibility and initiative. Any attempt to get out of the rut led to trouble." Now Colonel Richard Meinertzhagen, C.B.E., D.S.O., he lives in Kensington, with the great ensign of the *Königsberg* hanging on a wall and with his own telegraphic address—*Montezuma, London.*

The Belgians got control of the Ruanda Urundi but not of the Tabora area, the Portuguese got back their small chunk of disputed territory at the mouth of the Rovuma, and the British gained control over the remainder of German East. It is that latter, and largest, part of what was once a German colony cut out of Africa by Lord Kitchener and others that has become the independent state of Tanganyika. Thus were the modern African states made.

BIBLIOGRAPHY

THE following three works were indispensable in the writing of this book:

Official History of the Great War—Military Operations—East Africa, Vol. I, Lt.-Colonel Charles Hordern (H.M.S.O., 1941).

My Reminiscences of East Africa, General P. von Lettow-Vorbeck (Hurst & Blackett, 1920). This work has been published in the United States under the title *East African Campaigns* (Robert Speller & Sons, 1957).

Army Diary, 1899–1926, Colonel R. Meinertzhagen (Oliver & Boyd, 1960).

The following were also most useful, and all quotations come from them and those above:

The South Africans with General Smuts in German East Africa, 1916, J. Collyer (Union of South Africa Govnt., 1939).

General Smuts's Campaign in East Africa, Brigadier-General J. H. V. Crowe (John Murray, 1918).

Trekking On, Deneys Reitz (Faber & Faber, 1933).

Blockade & Jungle, N. Kock (ed. C. P. Christensen), (Robert Hale, 1941).

East African Experiences 1916, C. W. S. Shackleton (Knox, Durban, 1940).

The Empire at War, Vol. IV, ed. Sir Charles Lucas (Oxford, 1926).

The Gold Coast Regiment in the East African Campaign, Sir Hugh Clifford (John Murray, 1920).

The East African Field Force, Brigadier-General C. P. Fendall (Witherby, 1921).

Life of F. C. Selous, J. G. Millais (Longmans, 1918).

Marching on Tanga, F. Brett Young (Collins, 1917).

With the Nigerians in German East Africa, W. D. Downes (Methuen, 1919).

Sketches of the East Africa Campaign, R. V. Dolbey (John Murray, 1918).

Three Years of War in East Africa, A. Buchanan (John Murray, 1919).

Kenya Chronicles, Lord Cranworth (Macmillan, 1939).

And All For What? D. W. J. Cuddeford (Heath Cranton, 1933).

The Great World War—A History, ed. F. A. Mumby (Gresham, 1920).

The following were also consulted, and were of much help:

Official History of the Great War—Naval Operations, Vols. I, II, IV, Sir J. S. Corbett and B. Newbolt (Longmans, 1920–31).

Official History of the Great War—Medical Services General History, Vol. IV, Major-General Sir W. G. Macpherson and T. J. Mitchell (H.M.S.O., 1924).

The King's African Rifles, H. Moyse-Bartlett (Gale & Polden, 1956).

K.A.R., W. Lloyd-Jones (Arrowsmith, 1926).

British Campaigns in Africa and the Pacific 1914–18, E. Dane (Hodder & Stoughton, 1919).

The War in Africa and in the Far East, H. C. O'Neill (Longmans, 1919).

The Royal Fusiliers in the Great War, H. C. O'Neill (Heinemann, 1922).

The Loyal North Lancashire Regiment, Vol. II, H. C. Wylly (R.U.S.I., 1933).

The Watery Maze, B. Fergusson (Collins, 1961).

The Story of a Lion Hunt, A. Wienholt (Melrose, 1922).

Ambush, W. E. Wynn (Hutchinson, 1937).

Jan Christian Smuts, J. C. Smuts (Cassell, 1952).

Grey Steel: J. C. Smuts, H. C. Armstrong (Arthur Barker, 1937).

Bulawayo, 102, 259

Bulawayo Chronicle, 264

Bulgaria, 109

Buller, Major, 146

Butler, Captain F. J. P., 154

Buttar, Commander von, 235

Byron, Lieutenant-Colonel the Hon. J. J., 118

Cairo, 34

Calcutta, 30

Cape to Cairo Railway, 102

Carew, Captain P. F., 173

"Carew's Flying Column," 122

Caulfield, Captain F. W., R.N., 43–48, 60

Central Railway (Dar-es-Salaam to Lake Tanganyika), 22, 28, 89, 146, 166, 170, 172, 178, 179, 199, 208, 211, 221, 257, 259; British thrust for, 127, 129, 131, 137–140, 146–150; capture of, 150

Chambezi River, 261

Chilembwe, John, 74

Chiwata, 222

Cole, Berkeley, 76

Columns in Portuguese East Africa, typical formation and conditions of, 246–249

Counterfeit currency, introduced by Meinertzhagen, 87

Cranworth, Lord, 75, 270

Crewe, Brigadier-General Sir Charles, 170–180

Cunliffe, Brigadier-General F. H. G., Commander of Nigerian Brigade, 195, 213

Dar-es-Salaam, 17, 64, 91, 146, 159, 162, 170, 187, 202, 210, 218, 231–232, 234, 241, 248, 249, 251, 257, 268; bombarded by the *Astraea,* 27; truce in, 44; bombarded by the *Fox,* 96; captured by the British, 163–165; inadequacy of the port, 192; van Deventer's H.Q. in, 210, 255–256

Dartnell, Lieutenant Wilbur, 81

Delamere, Lord, 27

Deventer, Brigadier-General J. L. (later General Sir Jacob Louis) van, 122, 127, 143, 144, 180, 188–191, 193, 227; Commander of S. African Expeditionary Force, 114, 115; leads 1st S.A. Mounted Brigade to Kondoa-Irangi, 129–138, 143–144; his great ability, 133–134; reaches Dodoma, 146–149; reaches Kilosa, 161–162; leaves Kilosa, 162; receives Order of St. Vladimir, 164; his supply problems, 199–200; Commander-in-Chief, East Africa, 209, 210; congratulated by the King and Haig, 231; asks for exchange of medical prisoners, 251; his staff, 255–256; advises von Lettow of Armistice, 261; entertains von Lettow, 268; later career, 269–270

Dickinson, Lieutenant-Colonel, 250, 262, 263

Disease, among the troops, 76, 183–184, 220–221, 252–253, 268; mortality from, 265–266

Dodoma, 146

Driscoll, Colonel D. P., 79, 99; quoted, 141

ABOUT THE AUTHOR

BRIAN GARDNER *was educated at Dublin University, and after a time as an army teacher became a Fleet Street journalist. He traveled the world for his newspaper, visiting fifty countries, but decided to give it up for the quieter life of full-time authorship when his first book,* The Big Push—*an account of the Battle of the Somme in the First World War—was chosen by the Book Society of England as its nonfiction choice for May 1961. The book was on the best-seller lists in England for two months. Mr. Gardner's family have helped settle Central Africa for four generations, and he has lived with the campaign in East Africa all his life: an uncle and several other relatives died in it. The author now lives in London with his wife, also a graduate of Dublin University, and his young son.*